VALOUR BEYOND ALL PRAISE

HARRY GREENWOOD VC

DEREK HUNT

Published by
Derek Hunt
Windsor, Berkshire

Copyright, Derek Hunt 2003
The moral right of the author has been asserted.

All rights reserved. No part of this publication may be reproduced, stored in a retrieval system or transmitted in any form or by any means, electronic, mechanical, photocopying, recording or otherwise, without the prior permission of the author.

ISBN: 0-9545871-0-3

Printed by:
The Chameleon Press Ltd.
5-25 Burr Road, Wandsworth, London SW18 4SQ

"His valour and leading during two days of fighting were beyond all praise."

The London Gazette 26 December 1918

Contents

Preface		vi
Foreword by Captain Richard W. Annand VC DL		vii
Acknowledgements		ix
A Short History of the Victoria Cross		xi
1	Early Life (1881-1899)	1
2	From Boer War to Great War	9
3	1914-1915	21
4	1916-1917	33
5	January-May 1918	43
6	June-October 1918	51
7	1918 Ovillers to Grand Gay Farm road	63
8	Victoria Cross	85
9	The Inter-War Years	95
10	Second World War	111
11	Post-War Years	121
12	Epilogue	127
Appendix I
Orders, Decorations and Medals awarded to Harry Greenwood VC		137
Appendix II
Victoria Cross winners of The King's Own Yorkshire Light Infantry		139
Sources and Bibliography		141
Index		146

Preface

I have long admired the courage and devotion to duty of Lieutenant-Colonel Harry Greenwood VC DSO* OBE MC, who was born in my home town of Windsor. He won the Victoria Cross, the nation's highest award for bravery, in 1918 during the closing stages of the Great War. The award was not for a single action but for his valour and leadership skills over a crucial two day period.

The idea for a book about him began in 1998 at the Windsor Victoria Cross Exhibition. So many visitors had expressed their admiration of Lt. Col. Greenwood's bravery and hoped that someone would write his biography that I decided to try and do justice to this little-known war hero.

I did not know then about the pitfalls which await the first time author otherwise I might have thought better of the idea. Harry Greenwood has not proved an easy man to write about. He left behind no diaries or letters, or anything which might assist a biographer. However, I have been very fortunate in having such a large number of individuals and organisations willing to assist me and my work has been made considerably easier thanks to them. Despite all this expert advice any errors or omissions within the text are my responsibility.

Harry Greenwood displayed incredible courage during his military career but was also a kind and considerate husband and father. I have tried to show both sides of this remarkable man. In addition I have attempted to record how he spent the last 29 years of his life, from receiving his Victoria Cross in 1919 to his untimely death in 1948, a period of which little was previously known. He is still held in high esteem by those who knew him, many of whom have contributed to this book, and I am delighted that his life story can, at last, be told.

DEREK HUNT
July 2003

Foreword

Captain Richard W. Annand VC DL

Second Lieutenant R W Annand receiving congratulations on being awarded the Victoria Cross from Pte. R Piper, who was one of his platoon in France. (photograph: Imperial War Museum BH 1193)

It is a great honour to be invited to write a foreword to an account of the life of such a highly distinguished soldier.

While I myself served in the Durham Light Infantry and Lieutenant-Colonel Greenwood in the King's Own Yorkshire Light Infantry our two regiments have fought side by side and now form part of the Light Infantry, so I feel we share the same Regiment now.

Lieutenant-Colonel Harry Greenwood was certainly among the bravest of the brave having been awarded the MC, the DSO, a bar to his DSO and finally the VC. Derek Hunt has written a most interesting account of his wonderful exploits which will, I am sure, be an inspiration to all who read it.

Richard Annand.

Acknowledgements

I am grateful to Major C. M. J. Deedes, Regimental Secretary, Light Infantry Office (Yorkshire), for all his assistance and his permission to use extracts from *History of the King's Own Yorkshire Light Infantry in the Great War 1914-1918* by Lt. Col. R. C. Bond. This regimental history has formed the foundation for the chapters relating to the First World War.

The National Archives, Kew (formerly the Public Record Office) have been very helpful in allowing the reproduction of extracts from the War Diaries of 9th Battalion the King's Own Yorkshire Light Infantry, 64th Infantry Brigade and others (full details can be found in the Sources section).

I am indebted to the staff of the following institutions, many of whom have allowed me to reproduce material from their archives: National Army Museum for access to the Canon Lummis VC Files (held on behalf of the Military Historical Society), RHQ Grenadier Guards, the Imperial War Museum, The King's Own Yorkshire Light Infantry Museum, the Royal Logistic Corps Regimental Museum, Bruce Castle Museum Tottenham, the Ministry of Defence, the Met Office, Putney Vale Cemetery, the Victoria Cross and George Cross Association, Wimbledon Library, Windsor Library and many others, listed under Sources.

Many of the maps reproduced in this book are from *History of the Great War, Military Operations France & Belgium 1914-1918* edited by Brigadier-General Sir James Edmonds, HMSO 1922-1949. Other maps were specially drawn by Dorien Clifford. Many of the photographs are reproduced by kind permission of the Imperial War Museum. The copyright owners of the other photographs used are acknowledged with the individual reproductions.

Many individuals have also been of great assistance and I would like to thank: Dorien Clifford, Alan Jordan, Mrs Rosamond Nicholls, Colonel Paul Oldfield, Mlle Claudine Pardon, Dennis Pillinger, Mrs Carol Scott, Mrs Ady Sheldon, Mr J. V. Webb and Lt. Col. Bob Wyatt MBE TD. Thanks are also due to Captain Richard Annand VC who wrote the foreword and John Mulholland who edited my finished draft and compiled the index. I am grateful to Gordon Hamlin and everyone at Chameleon Press for turning my manuscript into a finished book.

Harry Greenwood's family have been extremely helpful, particularly Cynthia List (Harry's daughter), John Greenwood, Charles Greenwood, Roland Greenwood and Mrs Patricia Roberts.

My own family has also been a great support and I should like to thank my father-in-law, Ronald Fisher, who acted as my driver during my recent ill health and my wife Barbara who typed up my handwritten manuscript and was always there to help me.

Thank you to everyone who took part in this project and without whom this book could never have been written. If I have inadvertently omitted to mention anyone who has helped me please accept my sincere apologies.

A Short History of the Victoria Cross

The Crimean War (1854-1856) had drawn attention to the inadequacies of the existing means of rewarding gallantry in action and it became apparent that a new award was required. As a result the Victoria Cross (VC) was instituted by a Royal Warrant dated 29 January 1856. It was, as Queen Victoria observed, not an Order and carried with it no knighthood or special privileges. The new award, to be called the Victoria Cross after the Queen, was "to be highly prized and eagerly sought after by the Officers and Men of Our Naval and Military Services."

Unlike previous decorations and medals the VC was to be awarded to all ranks - the only qualification being bravery in the presence of the enemy. Clause six of the Royal Warrant stated that "neither rank, nor long service, nor wounds, nor any other circumstance or condition whatsoever save the merit of conspicuous bravery" would be sufficient to deserve this high honour. Although instituted in January 1856, the award was made retrospective to the beginning of the Crimean War and the earliest deed of bravery to be rewarded was in June 1854. Charles Lucas, serving aboard HMS *Hecla* has the distinction of being the first VC recipient. The 20 year old Mate picked up a live shell, which had landed on the deck of the ship, and threw it overboard.

Since then it has been awarded to a total of 1,351 individuals, including the American Unknown Warrior. Three men have won the Victoria Cross twice and received a bar to the original cross rather than a second VC.

The design of the VC was chosen by Queen Victoria, who also chose the simple inscription "FOR VALOUR." This is on a scroll beneath the Royal Crest of a lion surmounting a crown on the obverse of the decoration. In 1902 King Edward VII allowed for awards to be made posthumously and in 1911 King George V extented eligibility to native officers and men of the Indian Army. In 1920 a further Royal Warrant included the newly formed Royal Air Force. The VC ribbon was originally red for the army and blue for the navy, but after the creation of the RAF it was decided not to introduce yet another colour and since 1920 all ribbons have been red. When the ribbon only is worn it has a miniature VC in the centre.

The Victoria Cross has been made by the same firm of jewellers, Hancocks & Co, since 1857. Each cross is made of bronze from cannons captured at Sebastopol during the Crimean War. Queen Victoria held the first investiture ceremony in Hyde Park, London in June 1857 when she made presentations to 62 VC recipients, including the first recipient, Charles Lucas. The Victoria Cross is the nation's highest award for valour and takes precedence over all other decorations and medals.

Chapter One

Early Life (1881-1899)

What would possess a soldier to charge an enemy machine-gun position, not once but several times, when the odds of survival are stacked against him? What makes a hero? Courage, certainly; but also determination and a very strong sense of duty.

For Lieutenant-Colonel Harry Greenwood there would have been no doubts about what had to be done when his battalion's advance was held up by a German machine-gun post on Wednesday 23 October 1918. Single-handed he rushed the enemy position, killed the gunners and moved on to the next machine-gun post. For this action, and others over a two day period, he was awarded the Victoria Cross, Britain's highest award for valour. He could have taken advantage of his rank and stayed out of harm's way, ordering his men to eliminate the deadly machine-gunners. But that would not have been Harry Greenwood's style - he always led from the front, setting an example that inspired the whole battalion. In the words of his VC citation - "His valour and leading during two days of fighting were beyond all praise."

Nor was this an isolated example of his outstanding courage. He had also been awarded the Military Cross in 1916 and the Distinguished Service Order, and Bar, earlier in 1918 - but the Victoria Cross was the ultimate accolade. Even with all these awards for bravery he would still not consider himself a hero. He was, he believed, only doing his duty. The War brought forward so many men prepared to do their duty and fight, and in many cases to die, for their country.

Dictionary definitions of hero include "a man distinguished by exceptional courage" and "a man who is idealised for possessing superior qualities." Harry Greenwood fits both of these definitions. A hero acts as an inspiration for others, especially in wartime, and by his example sets new standards for others to achieve.

It has been said that Harry Greenwood lacked imagination; he just could not see what dangers he was exposing himself to through his own brave actions. Whether true or not, he was certainly not unduly worried about risking his own life if it meant his battalion could move forward. He was a man of great enthusiasm, impetuosity, undoubted physical courage and, at times, a fierce temper. The VC recommendation in 1918 praised Greenwood's "utter contempt for danger *(which)* contributed greatly towards the success of the operations during the advance." From his first action at Hill 70 in September 1915, for which he was awarded the MC, to the events which won him the VC, less than three weeks from the end of the war, his bravery was unwavering.

Harry Greenwood's father, Charles Greenwood, was an army sergeant so the young Harry would have been familiar with the idea of military service and duty to his country from an early age. He was to fulfil this duty in three major wars during his lifetime.

Charles Greenwood was born on 5 November 1853 in the parish of St Mary in Nottingham. His father and grandfather were also named Charles and both came from Nottingham, where they ran a fish stall in the market place. At the time the young Charles joined the army, aged 21, on 1 September 1875 he was a plumber by trade. He enrolled in the Grenadier Guards at Nottingham for an initial period of 12 years with the regimental number 5016.

Promotion followed and he became a Lance-Corporal in February 1878. He was promoted to Corporal in June 1878, Lance-Sergeant in May 1879 and Sergeant in November 1879. He received his second class Certificate of Education in June 1876 and passed an Instructor of Musketry course in October 1880. Most of his military service was spent in the UK, but he was posted to Egypt for four months in 1882 and to Bermuda for 12 months from July 1890.

At the beginning of Queen Victoria's reign men had enlisted in the army for life but this later changed to a system of short service, with further time in the reserve. This meant that the British Army had the advantage of always having a reserve of trained men to call upon if needed in time of war. Life in the army may not have been easy but soldiers were generally better fed than most civilians, and there had not been a major conflict since the Indian Mutiny of 1857. It was against this background that Charles Greenwood extended his original 12 year period of service to 21 years on 8 September 1884.

He married Margaret Abernethy at Trinity Church, Marylebone, London on 2 October 1880. Margaret was born in a village near Birr in Co Tipperary, Ireland on 4 June 1855, the second of 11 children. The Abernethy family originally came from Morayshire, Scotland and arrived in Ireland with Prince William of Orange, for whom they fought at the Battle of the Boyne. Margaret travelled to London in the 1870s in search of work and was employed as a lady's maid to a Lady Henniker, whose husband was in the Guards, when she met and married Charles Greenwood.

Harry was the eldest of their nine children, and was born at Windsor Infantry Barracks on Friday 25 November 1881. The birth was registered by Charles Greenwood on 21 December.

The 2nd Battalion Grenadier Guards was stationed at Windsor at the time, having moved there during September 1881. Sergeant Charles Greenwood and his wife were living in cramped conditions within the barracks. There were no proper married quarters then and married soldiers had to make their own arrangements for accommodation for their families, usually renting rooms in the area. Because of his seniority Sergeant Greenwood was allowed to accommodate his family in the barracks, but they would have found little privacy. A blanket hanging

Harry Greenwood was born at Windsor Infantry Barracks 25 November 1881. This copy of his birth certificate records his name as Henry.

across the end of a room would have been all that separated them from other occupants.

The population of the Borough of New Windsor in 1881 was 12,273 and the census that year recorded a total of 644 men, women and children living in the Infantry Barracks. Windsor had been a garrison town for centuries before the barracks were built between 1797 and 1803, though previously it had been customary to billet soldiers in private houses and inns throughout the town. The Infantry and Cavalry barracks housed the soldiers engaged in ceremonial duties at Windsor Castle and protected the Queen's residence (as they still do). Windsor has been a royal residence since King William I decided to build a castle on the chalk cliff overlooking the River Thames, and the town was granted its Charter of Freedom by King Edward I in 1277. Late Victorian Windsor was a very different place from today. In common with other garrison towns it had a large number of ale-houses and brothels, as well as some of the worst slums in the country.

In 1881 when Harry Greenwood was born Queen Victoria was in the 45th year of her long reign and William Gladstone was her Prime Minister. Also born in 1881 were Alexander Fleming, Pablo Picasso and P. G. Wodehouse. That year Britain had signed the Treaty of Pretoria with the Boers which recognised the independence of the South African Republic of Transvaal, and there was a nationalist rising in Egypt under Arabi Pasha. The Natural History Museum, South Kensington opened in April while in America President James Garfield was fatally shot in July. Benjamin Disraeli, Earl of Beaconsfield, also died that year aged 77.

Harry's birth certificate records his first name as Henry, but he was known as Harry for most of his life. The Greenwood family left Windsor shortly afterwards. Although Harry only spent the first few months of his life in Windsor his birth, in view of his later achievements, was significant enough for the Royal Borough of Windsor and Maidenhead to erect a plaque at the barracks 116 years later.

Harry Greenwood was one of only two Victoria Cross winners to have been born in Windsor. The other was Alexander Hore-Ruthven, later 1st Earl of Gowrie. Hore-Ruthven was born at The Hermitage, Windsor in 1872 and returned, as Lord Gowrie, to become Governor of Windsor Castle in 1945. There is no recorded visit by Harry Greenwood as an adult to his town of birth.

During the 1880s Windsor Infantry Barracks were renamed Victoria Barracks, although they continued to be the home of infantry regiments from the Brigade of Guards. Raised in 1656 by the exiled King Charles II as his personal bodyguard, the Grenadier Guards were, and still are, the senior of the five Foot Guards regiments.

Charles Greenwood's battalion, and their families, moved to Cork, Ireland in February 1882. Harry was baptised (as Henry) at the Garrison Chapel in Cork on 28 March 1882 by the Rev. M. Cooke.

Sergeant Greenwood left for active service in Egypt with the Grenadier Guards at the end of July. Anglo-French control of Egypt was causing some unrest, particularly in the Egyptian Army which mutinied under the

The original infantry barracks in Victoria Street, Windsor built in 1795. (Photograph copyright of the Royal Borough Museum Collection)

Victoria Barracks today. The old buildings were demolished and a new barracks built in the 1980s. (Photograph: Derek Hunt)

control of Colonel Ahmed Arabi. This triggered an anti-European uprising and in 1882 Khedive Tewfik of Egypt appealed to Britain and France for help. An Anglo-French expedition was planned, but France later withdrew its support, and in July 1882 the Royal Navy bombarded the port of Alexandria. This was followed up by a successful British invasion which suppressed the nationalist uprising. A grateful Khedive Tewfik conferred the Khedive's Star on those members of the British forces who qualified for the Egypt Medal. Sergeant Greenwood, who received both medals, returned to the UK to be reunited with his family at Chelsea Barracks, London in November 1882.

Battalions of the Brigade of Guards were normally rotated every six months. During the 1880s Charles Greenwood's battalion was frequently moved between Wellington Barracks London, Chelsea Barracks, The Tower, Windsor and Dublin. In October 1888 the Greenwood family returned to Victoria Barracks, Windsor with the battalion. They remained there until October 1889.

Following a collective act of disobedience the 2nd Battalion Grenadier Guards was posted to Bermuda in 1890. Because of the heat, humidity, and risk of tropical disease, Bermuda had never been a popular posting for any regiment. On 7 July 1890 the battalion, which was stationed at Wellington Barracks, London, failed to present themselves on parade as ordered. This was regarded as extremely serious, almost an act of mutiny, and at a Court Martial men from each company were convicted and imprisoned. The rest of the battalion, as punishment, was posted to Bermuda and sailed on 22 July 1890. They remained at the Royal Barracks, St George's until September 1891, although Sergeant Charles Greenwood is known to have returned to the UK in July 1891, having been away just over one year. The battalion was very fortunate to have been brought home so quickly. Soldiers sent to that disease-ridden colony often stayed for many years.

Regimental records reveal that families did not accompany the men on this posting, although it has long been believed in the Greenwood family that Margaret and some of the younger children also went to Bermuda. It would not have been too difficult for Charles Greenwood, as a senior NCO, to arrange passage for his family and find them local lodgings. Margaret was often quoted as saying that the Bermuda trip was one of the happiest times of her life. Harry, aged eight at the time the battalion departed from England, remained behind and is said to have been boarded with neighbours.

Not much is known about Harry Greenwood's early life and this period is less well documented than some of the more famous VC recipients. Because of the nomadic nature of army life Harry was seldom in one location long enough to attend school regularly. Consequently, he did not receive a formal education and was (as he later wrote in his *Who's Who* entry) "educated privately."

School photographs and reports are non-existent and it is believed that he received only a rudimentary education. He achieved no scholastic qualifications, nor did he aspire to university entrance. However, this did not prevent him from making his mark in later life. He was intelligent, resourceful and able to rise to any new challenge. Some of his younger brothers and sisters were more fortunate in receiving a regular schooling when Charles left the army and the family settled in one place.

Large families were not uncommon in Victorian times, and after the birth of Harry in 1881 Charles and Margaret were to have a further eight children. Their names and dates of birth are recorded in the family bible:

Maria Annette	born	12 January 1883
Margaret	born	14 August 1884
Charles	born	3 July 1886
Arthur	born	18 June 1888
David	born	13 March 1890
Kate	born	20 November 1892
Mary Ann	born	1 December 1894
John	born	14 September 1897

With so many siblings, as well as the large families of other soldiers around him, Harry would never have been without friends, and at times the barracks must have been as lively as any school playground. In Windsor, for example, the 1881 census showed there were 77 children of various ages living in the barracks.

Charles Greenwood left the army in September 1896, having completed his 21 years with the Grenadier Guards. During his military service he had received the Egyptian Medal 1882 and the Khedive's Bronze Star, in addition to the Medal for Long Service and Good Conduct. (The current whereabouts of these medals are unknown.)

The Greenwood family settled in Tottenham, north London in 1896. From the 1870s, with the opening of the local railway, this rural town in Middlesex had become a popular area for artisans and working class commuters. Rents were relatively low and large areas of terraced housing were built as the town grew, and it eventually became a suburb of London. *Kelly's Directory* records the Greenwood family living at 35 Westerfield Road, Tottenham in 1898. By 1901 they had moved to 235 Park Lane.

After leaving the army Charles Greenwood returned to his former trade as a plumber. He was later to become a Yeoman of the Guard, the ranks of which were usually filled by former soldiers.

The young Harry enjoyed reading Kipling and later in life quoted from his favourite works. Rudyard Kipling was very popular with his generation. He received the Nobel Prize for Literature in 1907 and was regarded as the poet of the Empire. Harry was particularly fond of *Stalky and Co*, based on Kipling's schooldays, and liked to identify himself with 'Stalky'; as the elder brother full of cunning ruses and tricks. Not surprisingly, 'Stalky' became his family nickname.

Queen Victoria's Diamond Jubilee in 1897 saw the zenith of Great Britain's overseas Empire and the Jubilee was triumphantly celebrated around the world. It is said that the past is another country. Things were certainly very different then and it seemed that the sun would never set on the British Empire. Soldiers, as well as Empire builders such as Cecil Rhodes, were the heroes of the time - not the pop stars and footballers of today. With such role models as Lord Roberts VC and Lord Kitchener it is not surprising that the army was a popular choice as a career for many young men.

Harry Greenwood was keen to follow his father into the army and on 21 July 1897, aged 15, he joined the 1st Cadet Battalion, King's Royal Rifle Corps based at Finsbury Square, east London. He joined as cadet number 1401. (After leaving the Grenadier Guards Charles Greenwood was appointed Sergeant-Major of this Cadet Corps.) At the time Harry was working as an apprentice compositor with *The Times* at Printing House Square, in the City. He proved to be an able army cadet and by 1899 had attained the rank of Sergeant. This military experience enabled him to take an active role in the impending conflict in South Africa. The other four Greenwood boys joined the cadet battalion, at the drill hall in Sun Street, as soon as they became old enough - it was a matter of duty.

Chapter Two

From Boer War to Great War

The South African War of 1899-1902, also known as the Boer War, began in October 1899. What had started as the last colonial war of the Victorian era ended as the first modern war of the 20th century.

Tension had been mounting between Britain and the Boer republics of the Transvaal and Orange Free State since both former colonies had gained independence. The Boers, originally Dutch settlers, felt threatened by the British presence in South Africa and what they considered to be political interference in their internal affairs. War became inevitable when Britain ignored a Boer ultimatum it could not be expected to accept.

Paul Kruger, the President of the Transvaal, warned that unless British troops in Natal were withdrawn from the borders of the Boer republics, and reinforcements halted, a state of war would exist. On Thursday 12 October 1899 Transvaal Boer Commandos invaded Natal. Their plan was to advance to the coast before further British reinforcements could arrive but it was blocked by stronger than expected forces and the determined defence of Ladysmith. The towns of Kimberley and Mafeking in Cape Colony were also besieged by the Boers.

A series of British defeats at Magersfontein, Stormberg and Colenso in December 1899 shook the establishment and brought about much needed changes in the way the war was fought. The veteran soldier Field Marshal Lord Roberts VC was appointed Commander-in-Chief in South Africa and Lord Kitchener, who had conquered the Sudan the previous year, became his Chief-of-Staff. Large numbers of reinforcements from Britain, Australia, Canada and other parts of the Empire were promised and started to arrive at the Cape in January 1900.

Harry Greenwood was only 17 when hostilities began (he was 18 the following month) but tried to enlist in a regiment going to South Africa. Having been brought up in a military family he was eager for adventure and the chance to serve his country. In this his father would not have tried to dissuade him. The War Office received numerous offers of assistance from the Volunteer Battalions, which had been raised for local service. These offers were all declined. However, after the disasters of what became known as 'Black Week' in December 1899 the Commander-in-Chief of the Army, Lord Wolseley, accepted an offer of help from the Lord Mayor of London. A plan was quickly put into operation, and later that month Greenwood applied to join the City of London Imperial Volunteers (CIV) which were soon to leave for the Cape Colony.

This new regiment was raised by drawing marksmen from all the Volunteer Battalions of the capital, including The King's Royal Rifle Corps

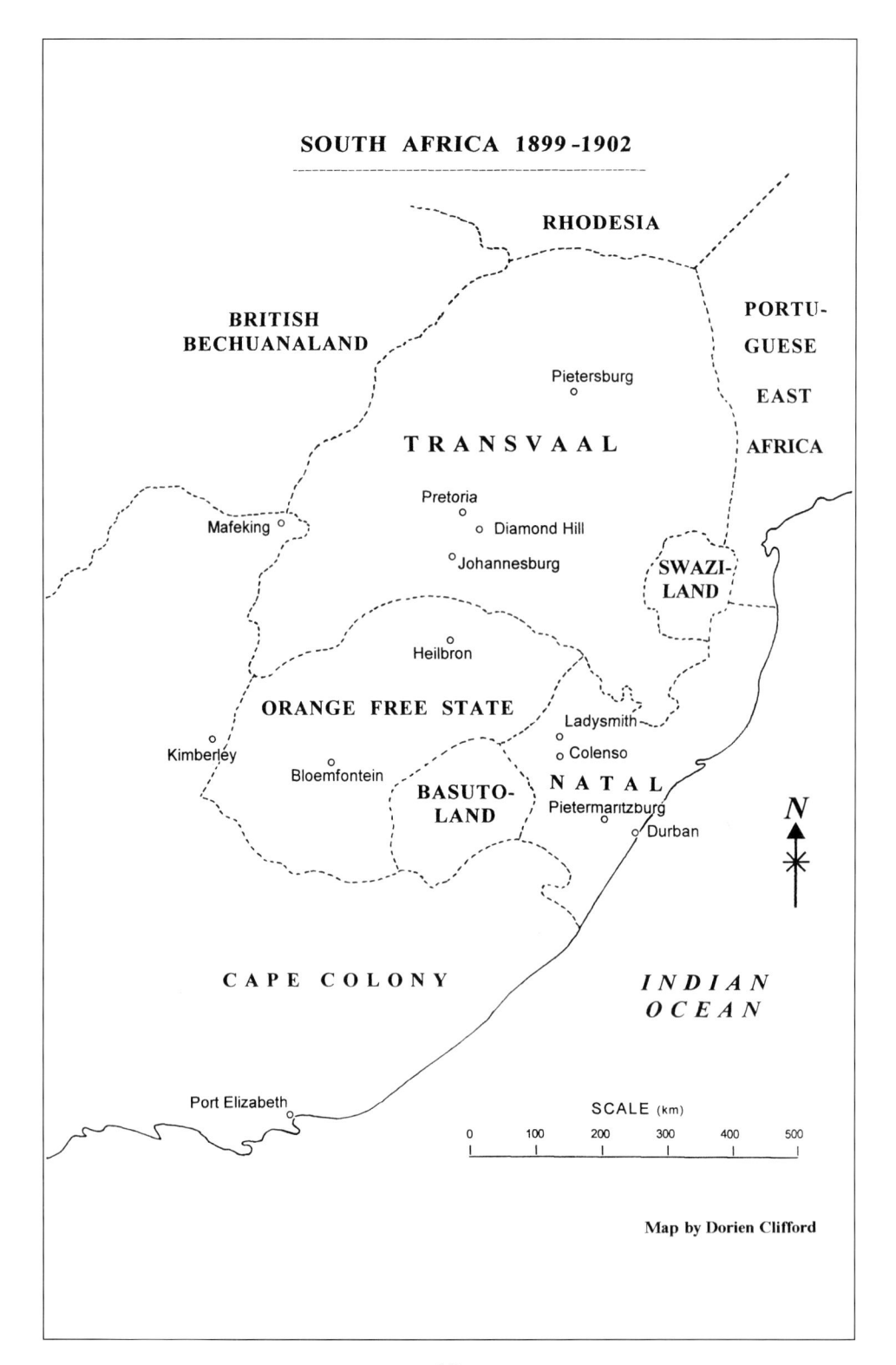

SOUTH AFRICA 1899-1902

Map by Dorien Clifford

(KRRC) Cadets which contributed 15 men to the Infantry Battalion. The CIV was established from a total of 53 Volunteer Battalions, which had been formed for home defence. Colonel Commandant of the regiment was Colonel W. H. Mackinnon, a former Grenadier Guards officer.

In December 1899 all Volunteer units in the London area had been instructed to forward details of not more than 40 suitable men who wished to be considered for the CIV. Harry Greenwood was one of those chosen from these lists. He was then only 18, when the lowest official age for service in South Africa was 20, but had stated his age as "20 years and one month." It is likely, in view of the number of other recruits claiming to be 20 enlisting from the KRRC Cadets, that he was not the only underage volunteer. He had given his occupation on joining as "compositor."

1ST CADET BATTALION KING'S ROYAL RIFLES.
C.I.V.

First Row (standing).—Staff-Sergt Sherwood; Sergt. Greenwood; Sergt. Bailey; Corpl. Barrett; Col.-Sergt. Lancaster; Sergt. Faith; Sergt. Trussler.
Second Row (sitting).—Col. Sergt. Faith; Col.-Sergt. Nicol; Sergt. Fitzpatrick; Col.-Sergt. Ellett; Sergt. Coombe; Col.-Sergt. Hutchins.

Reproduced from *The Transvaal in Peace and War*, 1900.

1ST **CADET BATTALION KING'S ROYAL RIFLES.**

Headquarters—2, Finsbury Square, E.C.   *Commanding Officer*—Lieut.-Col. Freeman Williams.

Colr.-Sergt. E. H. Nightingale   Colr.-Sergt. B. H. Nicol   Sergeant A. W. Faith   Sergeant H. Greenwood   Corporal J. Barrett
,, F. E. Lancaster   Sergeant T. W. Trussler   ,, R. E. Coombe   Ambulance Staff-Sergeant   Lance-Corporal E. G. Henneman
,, K. E. Ellett   ,, W. Hutchings   ,, F. F. Bailey   E. C. Sherwood
,, F. H. Faith   ,, J. Fitzpatrick

The Text and all the Portraits and other Illustrations in this Souvenir are copyright. (V. E. & L. Collingridge, London).

Reproduced from *City Press*, CIV Souvenir.

Volunteers were enrolled at the Guildhall starting on 1 January 1900. Regrettably, none of these enlistment papers still exist; they were all destroyed during the Blitz. Each man was given a newly minted shilling and the Freedom of the City. (Greenwood's number on the City of London Corporation Freedom Roll was 851.) They left for South Africa later that month via Southampton where the Lord Mayor, Sir Alfred Newton, bade them farewell.

In addition to the Freedom of the City of London, all members of the CIV received a commemorative swagger cane with a silver top incorporating the arms of the City of London and the initials CIV. Greenwood's cane is now held at The King's Own Yorkshire Light Infantry Museum in Doncaster.

Private Greenwood served with the CIV throughout the unit's time in South Africa - February to October 1900. On arrival the CIV was attached to the 21st Brigade under Major-General Bruce Hamilton. Lord Roberts VC, as a sign of his respect for the CIV, became the Regiment's honorary Colonel in March 1900.

The Volunteers served alongside regular troops, as well as other units such as the Imperial Yeomanry, and were frequently in the forefront of the fighting. Uniforms, paid for by the City of London Corporation, were similar with Volunteer units wearing Australian style slouch hats. Other ranks were not, however, issued their standard khaki uniforms until the day before they sailed. (Harry Greenwood's slouch hat, brought home as a souvenir, was to end its days as a gardening hat for his father Charles who wore it while digging his allotment.)

A contemporary postcard showing the CIV infantry battalion in uniform.

Although he had been a sergeant in the Cadet Corps Greenwood, like others, had to relinquish his rank when joining the CIV as there was an over-subscription of volunteers. The total strength of the new unit was 64 officers and 1,675 other ranks.

After reaching Capetown in mid-February the CIV began a long march through the Orange Free State and crossed the Vaal River into Transvaal at the end of May. An action at Doorn Kop, which included the 21st Brigade, qualified the CIV for the 'Johannesburg' clasp on the Queen's South Africa Medal. Elsewhere in the war the towns of Ladysmith, Kimberley and Mafeking - which had all been besieged by the Boers - were relieved.

THE CITY IMPERIAL VOLUNTEERS IN A RECONNAISSANCE NEAR BRITSTOWN.

The Dutch element in Cape Colony gave great trouble during the days of Lord Roberts' inaction after Paardeberg. Lord Kitchener was sent to Prieska on March 2 to deal with the rebels in that district. At Britstown a party of Boers raided cattle, and on March 6 the 24th Battery R.F.A. with six guns, a company of the Warwickshire Mounted Infantry, and two companies of the C.I.V. were sent to disperse them, which they did with trifling loss.

Reproduced from *With the Flag to Pretoria*, Harmsworth Brothers Ltd 1900.

In June 1900 Harry Greenwood took part in the fierce fighting at Diamond Hill, in Transvaal, when a combined British force attacked this strategic Boer position. Together with battalions from the Sussex and Derbyshire Regiments the CIV advanced up the rocky slopes. Despite heavy enemy fire they captured the ridge, on 11 June, only to discover another and steeper ridge beyond, from where the Boers were firing at them. The British troops took cover and bivouaced there overnight, and the next day advanced further up the hill supported by reinforcements from the Brigade of Guards.

Forcing their way up to the summit the attacking force captured this second ridge but found that beyond it, and looking down upon it, was a third ridge held by the Boers. Taking cover among the rocks on this plateau

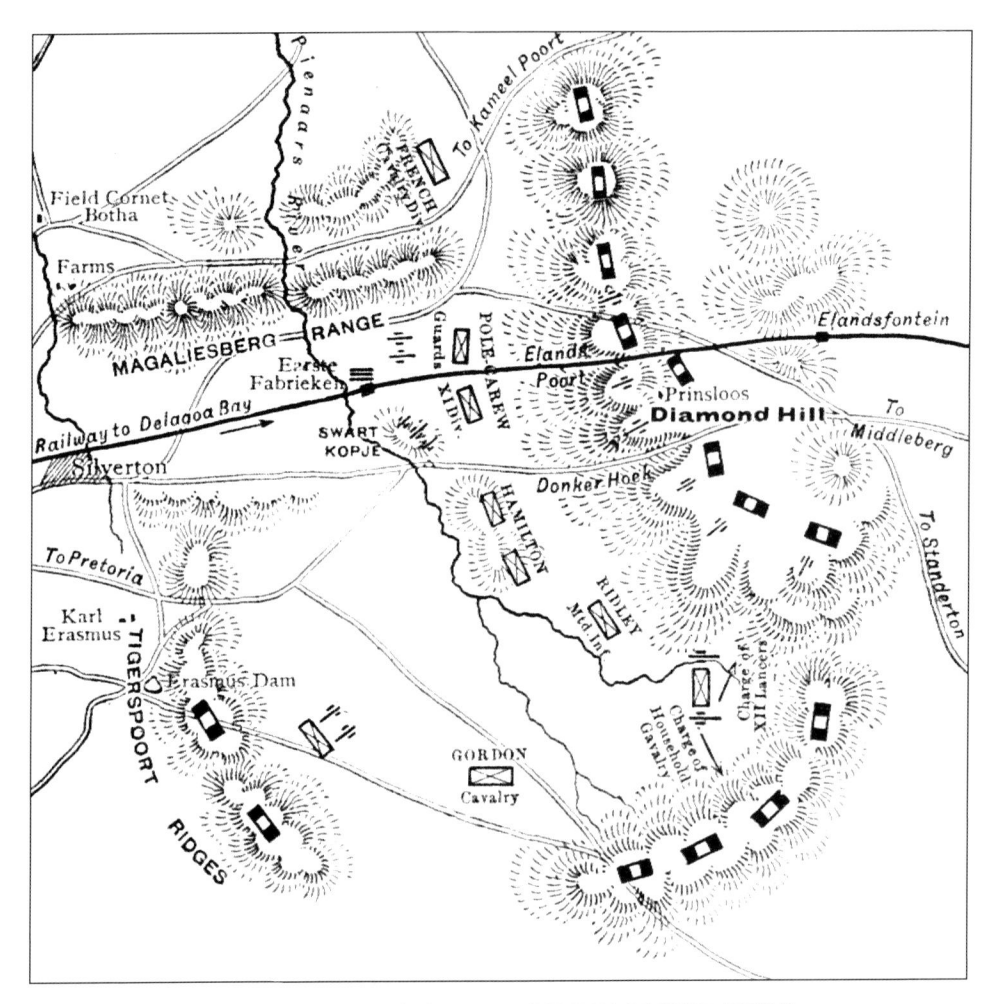

PLAN OF THE BATTLE OF DIAMOND HILL

Map reproduced from *With the Flag to Pretoria*, Harmsworth Brothers Ltd 1900.

the CIV waited for the Guards to follow them up the hill. The arrival of a British Field Artillery battery on the plateau inflicted heavy losses on the Boers, but failed to shift them from their ridge. It was a mounted infantry charge on a position at the foot of the hill that assured British victory. The Boers withdrew during the night, but it had taken two days to capture Diamond Hill. For his part in this action Harry Greenwood received a 'Diamond Hill' clasp to his Queen's South Africa Medal. Pretoria, the Transvaal capital, was captured by Lord Roberts on 5 June and the CIV later paraded through the city centre. The regiment subsequently served at Heilbron and Johannesburg.

Many of the Volunteer and Colonial units were in South Africa for pre-determined periods and trouble was encountered in October 1900 when some of the Colonial troops refused to serve beyond that time. Their real task was completed by then. Lord Roberts decided to send home all the Volunteer and Colonial troops, including the CIV, immediately. London enthusiastically welcomed back its own Volunteer regiment on its return from South Africa at the end of October. Huge crowds gathered to see the regiment march through the streets of the capital from Paddington Station to St Paul's Cathedral, where a service of thanksgiving was held. Colonel Mackinnon, Colonel Commandant of the regiment, wrote an official history *The Journal of the CIV in South Africa*. Greenwood is listed in the appendix showing the "list of NCOs and men of the regiment when first formed."

Harry Greenwood could easily have returned home with the CIV and received a hero's welcome, but he was determined not to leave until the job was finished. He was also enjoying himself too much to be in any hurry to go back home. It was the first time he had been abroad, the scenery in South Africa was spectacular and he had made some good friends out there. He arranged a transfer into the South African Light Horse (SALH) and served with that unit from October 1900 until June 1901. When he had applied to join the CIV less than 12 months earlier, Greenwood had "no knowledge of riding" and this was indicated on his enrolment form. But he had added two years to his age, so it is likely that he also exaggerated his riding ability when he transferred to the SALH.

This mounted unit had been raised at the Cape in November 1899, some 600 strong, and served in every theatre of the war. They were known as 'The Sakabulas' because of the distinctive long black tail feathers of the sakabula bird the men wore on their slouch hats. Winston Churchill, who went to South Africa as a war correspondent for *The Morning Post,* had received a commission as a Lieutenant in the South African Light Horse in January 1900. He wrote about his adventures in the SALH in his autobiography *My Early Life.*

After the British capture of Pretoria, in June 1900, the Boers were effectively beaten on the battlefield and Transvaal was annexed as a Crown Colony. Lord Roberts prematurely concluded that the war was over and began to make plans for reducing the role of the army and replacing it with a police force. However, he had underestimated the determination of the Boers, who were to fight a guerilla war for a further two years. A controversial policy of farm burning succeeded in depriving the guerillas of food and shelter, and the equally controversial imprisonment in 'concentration camps' of Boer families helped to wear down their resistance.

Greenwood transferred to the South African Constabulary (SAC) in June 1901. This unit was formed in October 1900, on the instructions of Lord Roberts, by Major-General Robert Baden-Powell, the hero of Mafeking. Roberts himself returned to England, leaving Lord Kitchener in command. With much of the Transvaal and Orange Free State and the inter-connecting railway system in British hands, army numbers were further reduced for what was considered a police operation. The South African Constabulary, commonly known as the Baden-Powell Police, took volunteers from other units and reached its target of 10,000 men in January 1902. Many former CIV men re-joined in the ranks of the SAC. The pay of five shillings a day for a private was considerably better than the one shilling a day paid at the time to privates in the regular army.

Most of the duties of the new police force involved guarding blockhouses, or fortified positions. Lines of blockhouses were constructed across the country and the lines were moved forward and new blockhouses built as British troops cleared the surrounding areas of guerillas. The SAC also escorted armoured trains, protecting them from attack by the Boers. During the war the use of mounted infantrymen proved highly successful. After the war the South African Constabulary served as the police force of the Orange Free State, the Transvaal and Swaziland.

While with this mounted unit Greenwood was involved in a riding accident. The nineteen-year-old was an inexperienced rider and, when on duty, was thrown by his horse. He was injured when the horse rolled on him and, much to his annoyance, was invalided home in October 1901. This was the end of Greenwood's South African military service. The next time he returned to South Africa was as private secretary to a wealthy industrialist.

The Treaty of Vereeniging in May 1902 brought a close to the war, with the Boers accepting British sovereignty. Britain and her Empire allies suffered over 21,000 fatalities, mostly from disease and inadequate hospital facilities. Queen Victoria had died in January 1901 and was succeeded by her son Edward VII.

When the South African War ended it was realised that men who had fought for nearly three years were to receive the same medal as men who had served for only a few months. King Edward, who was anxious to reward those who had served him well, ordered that an additional medal should be issued as a visible token of long service. The conditions were that the recipient should have served in South Africa in a military capacity for at least eighteen months between October 1899 and May 1902 and that he must have served in South Africa during the first five months of 1902.

Greenwood was awarded two South Africa medals. His Queen's South Africa Medal (QSA) had four clasps (the maximum number for the CIV Infantry Battalion) - Cape Colony, Orange Free State, Johannesburg and Diamond Hill. He also received the King's South Africa Medal (KSA) with two clasps - South Africa 1901 and South Africa 1902.

He should have served in South Africa during 1902 in order to qualify for the 1902 clasp, and the KSA itself, but as he did not return after October 1901 he should instead have received a South Africa 1901 clasp to his Queen's South Africa Medal. In his own *Who's Who* entry some years later Harry Greenwood recorded that he "served *(in the)* South African War 1899-1901." There appears to be no evidence that he served beyond October 1901 other than the South Africa 1902 clasp.

It is not known why he did not receive a South Africa 1901 clasp to his QSA, but there does appear to be some dispute about his length of service. The medal rolls at the National Archives conflict with information held by the Ministry of Defence (MoD). Harry Greenwood is shown on the medal rolls as serving with the Transvaal Provisional Police from 27 September 1900 until 5 March 1901, whereas MoD records show that he was with the South African Light Horse for most of this period and later served with the SAC until October 1901. He is not shown in any of the medal rolls as entitled to or receiving the KSA.

A close examination of the KSA, which is now held with his VC and other medals at The King's Own Yorkshire Light Infantry Museum in Doncaster, reveals that it is named to "1401 Pte. H. Greenwood CIV" (the same wording as his QSA). The KSA, as with most awards, was named to the recipient with the rank and unit in which he was serving when he earned the medal. Since the CIV was disbanded in November 1900 it is extremely unlikely that a KSA would be officially named to that unit. (1401 was Greenwood's number in The King's Royal Rifle Corps.) The lettering on the rim of the medal does not display the regular line of an officially struck naming.

It is almost certain that this medal was self-awarded. Greenwood may have believed that he was entitled to it as he had served in South Africa for most of 1901 and, when he did not receive the KSA officially, obtained one through unofficial means. It would appear that he bought another man's medal and, having had the original name removed, had his name engraved on the rim. He would not, however, have done this in order to deceive others. Harry Greenwood was a man of integrity, but he may have felt he had been denied a medal he fully deserved. He probably saw many of his friends returning from South Africa with both QSA and KSA medals and been unaware of the very strict rules for issuing campaign medals. This in no way diminishes his outstanding service to his country in three wars.

Official or not, Greenwood continued to wear the KSA ribbon on his uniform even when he received his VC from the King. Although no member of the CIV won the Victoria Cross many later served in the First World War and Harry Greenwood is the only former CIV man to receive this award.

Greenwood had met his future employer, Robert Williams, in 1901 while serving with the South African Constabulary. Williams had huge interests in mining and railways throughout southern Africa and had been working with Cecil Rhodes on the Cape to Cairo Railway. One of the main tasks of the SAC was to protect the armoured trains that criss-crossed the countryside, and it was while on escorting duties that Greenwood met Robert Williams and began a working relationship that was to last for the next 37 years.

After the war Greenwood's interest in the army continued and he rejoined his old Volunteer Battalion, The King's Royal Rifle Corps (KRRC) as Colour Sergeant. He was later appointed Sergeant-Instructor of Musketry and served in the volunteer/territorial units of the KRRC and the London Rifle Brigade until 1909. (Both regiments are now part of The Royal Green Jackets.) He remained on the Officers Reserve List until the start of the First World War in 1914.

At the time Harry joined the CIV he had listed his father, Charles Greenwood, as next of kin and the family home was then 235 Park Lane, Tottenham, north London. This house was said to have been haunted, but only Harry's mother had sharp enough senses to detect anything. Margaret Greenwood sensed atmospheres and was said to be able to 'hear' the ghost walking about the house on many occasions.

The family moved, in 1904, to rented accommodation at 2 West Road, Tottenham. A few years later they were able to buy this terraced house when Margaret received an inheritance from one of her relatives. In 1908 they moved out of London to a smallholding at Medstead, near Alton in Hampshire. Charles and Margaret set up a business raising chickens in order to sell eggs and tablefowl but the venture was shortlived as it was not a commercial success. Although he was good at raising fowls, Charles was no businessman and was unable to relate his production costs to profitable selling prices. The Greenwood family left Medstead and moved back to their house in West Road, Tottenham in 1909. Harry did not accompany his parents to Medstead as he had moved out of the family home by then.

Charles and Margaret remained at West Road, apart from when Charles was away on war service, until their deaths in the 1920s. Up until 1915, when he rejoined the army, Charles Greenwood was a member of the Yeoman of the Guard, based at St James's Palace in London. He told some interesting and often amusing stories about his work and what went on at State Banquets. Formed by Henry VII as his personal bodyguard in 1485, the duties of the Yeoman of the Guard are now purely ceremonial. They are distinct from the Yeoman Warders of the Tower of London. Charles was one of the Yeomen who kept watch at King Edward VII's lying-in-state in Westminster Hall in 1910. In acknowledgement of his services he was given a large framed engraving of the late King signed by King George V with the message "In memory of your vigil." This was proudly displayed in the Tottenham house and given to Harry after the death of his parents.

A few years before his marriage in 1909 Harry had suffered appendicitis, and while in hospital was looked after by a nurse named Helena. Her soothing attention soon helped to ease the pain and discomfort. They kept in touch after his discharge from hospital, and later fell in love and decided to marry. Harry's future wife, Helena Emily Anderson, was the eldest daughter of Daniel Gillespie Anderson and Helena Anderson, formerly Cracknew, from Newcastle-upon-Tyne. Helena was born on 14 March 1878, although she would later in life claim to have been born in March 1882. She was born at the then family home in Ashburton Crescent, Gosforth in Northumberland. Her father described himself on the birth certificate as an "agent for an Indian Rubber Company."

The marriage of Harry Greenwood and Helena Anderson took place at St Clement Danes Church, Strand, London on Saturday 9 January 1909. The register was in the name of, and signed by, Henry Greenwood - his name at birth. The name Harry does not appear on official documents until at least 1914. He listed his occupation as "secretary and mining engineer."

Harry Greenwood married Helena Anderson on 9 January 1909. Copy of their marriage certificate.

Helena Emily Anderson was born 14 March 1878. This copy of her birth certificate shows she was older than the 27 years claimed when she married Harry Greenwood.

Both bride and groom were said to be aged 27 at the time. Harry was 27 but Helena was in fact almost four years older than him. Another oddity was that Helena's father, Daniel Anderson, was shown in the register as Douglas.

At the time of the wedding both Harry and Helena were living at the Howard Hotel, Norfolk Street, east London. The marriage was to last for 39 years, until Harry's premature death in 1948.

Harry and Helena had four children. A son was born in July 1915 but died tragically when only a few days old from what today might have been called 'cot death syndrome.' At the time infant deaths were quite common from a number of causes. The boy, named Harry Charles Gillespie, was only four days old when he died and is buried in Tottenham Cemetery near to the plot where Charles and Margaret Greenwood were later laid to rest.

There were three daughters. The eldest daughter, Mollie Helena Margaret, was born on Friday 10 April 1914. At the time the family were living at 'Cantley,' Connaught Avenue, Chingford, Essex. Harry had registered the birth, giving his occupation as "private secretary." Mollie was followed three years later by Alice Stella Evelyn who was born on Saturday 7 July 1917, and the third daughter, Violet Cynthia Marion, was born on Tuesday 1 April 1919.

When he returned to England from South Africa Harry Greenwood worked in commerce as private secretary to Robert Williams. Born in Aberdeen in 1860, Robert Williams went out to Kimberley, South Africa, in 1881 to seek his fortune. There he met Cecil Rhodes (1853-1902) for whom he worked, initially, as an adviser in his many mining operations. Rhodes, the son of a Hertfordshire clergyman, had gone to South Africa for health reasons. His involvement in diamond mining made him a millionaire and he later entered politics, becoming Prime Minister of Cape Colony in 1890. He was fiercely patriotic and his ambition was to form a South African Dominion under British rule.

Williams had studied mining and geology and he and Cecil Rhodes formed the Zambesia Exploring Co Ltd and Tanganyika Concessions Ltd. With his substantial interests in Africa Williams made frequent visits, often accompanied by his private secretary. Greenwood remained with the Robert Williams & Co group of companies until 1914 and was back in England at the outbreak of war.

Chapter Three

1914-1915

The First World War, or The Great War as it was known at the time, began in August 1914. From a British viewpoint it was to be the most traumatic conflict in history. Years of unprecedented military build-up prior to 1914 combined with nationalistic fervour and the division of Europe into hostile alliances created a dangerous situation. All the major powers had expected war and were preparing for it.

For the previous ten years Germany had been planning how to fight a war on two fronts. In what became known as the 'Schlieffen Plan' the German Chief-of-Staff Alfred von Schlieffen proposed a strategic strike against France through Belgium and the rapid capture of Paris. France would then collapse and German troops could move quickly to the Eastern Front before the Russian army was fully mobilised. Speed was imperative in order to block any threat from Great Britain.

In such a highly charged situation it would not take much to spark a war. On Sunday 28 June 1914 Archduke Franz Ferdinand of Austria-Hungary and his wife were assassinated in Sarajevo, the capital of Bosnia. The shots fired that day by Gavrilo Princip, a Bosnian student, set in motion a series of events which five weeks later led to war. Austria-Hungary held Serbia responsible for supporting the terrorist group behind the assassinations, broke off diplomatic relations and began to mobilise its army for war. Russia, a long time protector of Serbia, mobilised in response and as a warning to Austria-Hungary not to invade Serbia. Germany, calculating that war had finally arrived, issued an ultimatum to Russia that if it did not demobilise within 12 hours a state of war would exist. This warning was ignored and war became inevitable. Germany declared war on Russia on 1 August. Following the long proposed Schlieffen timetable of war Germany then declared war on France on 3 August and commenced the invasion.

Britain became involved when German troops entered Belgium as part of the encircling attack on France. Belgian neutrality was guaranteed by a British treaty of 1839 and Britain declared war on Germany on Tuesday 4 August 1914.

The advance guard of the British Expeditionary Force (BEF), under the command of Field Marshal Sir John French, arrived in France within a week. Britain was one of the few European countries not to use conscription and had instead a relatively small volunteer army of professional fighting men. The plan was for the British Army to assist its French and Belgian allies hold the line against the German advance. All army reserves were called up and in the jingoistic mood of the time it was confidently predicted that the war would "be over by Christmas."

Lord Kitchener, the Secretary of State for War, was less optimistic that the war would be so short-lived and planned for a longer campaign. He appealed for 100,000 volunteers to come forward and serve in the 'New Armies.' Recruiting stations were flooded with volunteers and by the end of 1914 over a million men had answered his call. Britain's main strength at the outbreak of war was its Navy, which was then the largest in the world.

During the first few months of the war it was a relatively fast moving conflict and the system of trench warfare which was to characterise the war had not yet evolved. The BEF and its French Allies were forced to retreat from Mons, Belgium in late August 1914. Heavily outnumbered by the Germans, the Allied retreat continued to Le Cateau, France, close to the village of Ovillers where four years later Harry Greenwood would win the Victoria Cross. An Allied stand was made at the River Marne, only 20 miles from Paris, and the German advance halted. The German army was forced to withdraw to the heights above the River Aisne where it dug in. By the end of 1914 Allied and German trenches stretched from the Swiss border to the Belgian coast, a distance of approximately 450 miles.

At the outbreak of war Harry Greenwood, then aged 32, volunteered for active service. His first daughter, Mollie, had been born just four months earlier and he was enjoying family life, but like countless other men in the same position Greenwood knew where his duty lay. He was subsequently appointed to a Temporary Commission as Captain in the 9th (Service) Battalion of The King's Own Yorkshire Light Infantry (KOYLI).

The regiment had been raised as the 53rd Foot in 1755 but two years later was renamed Brudenell's, after its new Colonel, and renumbered 51st Foot. It served with distinction in the Seven Years War (1758-1764) and the Peninsula War. In 1839 the Honourable East India Company formed the 2nd Madras (European) Regiment. These two regiments became the 1st and 2nd Battalions of The King's Own Light Infantry (South Yorkshire Regiment) in 1881. In August 1914 the Regiment, now called The King's Own (Yorkshire Light Infantry), consisted of five battalions - two regular, one militia, and two territorial. Kitchener's call for volunteers led to the raising of six service battalions.

9th Battalion KOYLI had been formed as early as September 1914 with Lieutenant-Colonel R. C. Dill, a retired officer, as its first Commanding Officer. For the first twelve months of the war 9th KOYLI was busy recruiting and training. It was a huge undertaking to equip and train all the men rushing to join up, and in 1915 there was a shortage of qualified instructors. There was also a shortage of equipment and the battalion was at first issued with dummy rifles. It was not until July 1915 that every man received a serviceable rifle. The new battalion was attached to the 64th Infantry Brigade, which became part of the 21st Division. This division, part of the Third New Army, was to suffer more casualties than any other 'New Army' division during the war.

In October 1914 the 64th Infantry Brigade comprised of the 9th and 10th Battalions KOYLI and the 14th and 15th Battalions Durham Light Infantry (DLI). Although this constitution changed during the course of the war 9th KOYLI remained with the 64th throughout. Each battalion had a nominal strength of 1,000 officers and other ranks but actual numbers were usually nearer 800. The command structure at the time involved four battalions being grouped together to form a brigade. Three brigades formed a division, which was a self contained fighting force with its own artillery and support services. Two or more divisions were grouped together to form a corps, and two or more corps would form an army.

Originally raised at Pontefract, the 9th and 10th Battalions later moved to Berkhamstead and then Halton Park, Tring in October 1914. From November 1914 to April 1915 the new battalions were in billets in Maidenhead, Berkshire before moving back to Halton Park. They were inspected by HM The King as they marched through Windsor on their way to Witley Camp, Surrey in August. From Witley they made their way to France.

The Greenwood family circa 1915.
Back row: (left to right) Charles, Arthur, Harry, Margaret, Maria Baker
Front row: John, Ted Baker.

1915 was a year of frustration and mounting losses for the BEF and its allies. Earlier attempts to break through the German defences had largely failed. A British and Indian attack at Neuve Chapelle, in north east France, in March had captured a small area of ground, with heavy casualties, but German counter-attacks prevented further gains. At the Second Battle of Ypres, in Belgium, in April the Germans used poison gas for the first time - with devastating effect. An Allied attack on Aubers Ridge in May failed to capture the ridge beyond Neuve Chapelle and at Festubert later the same month a small territorial advance was made, but at great cost in British lives. The Germans were prepared to remain on the defensive, apart from offensives at Verdun and the Ypres Salient, until 1918.

Harry Greenwood received his first commission, as Temporary Captain in 9th KOYLI, on 4 April 1915. Many men who joined the 'New Armies' received temporary commissions, indicating that the appointment was for the duration of the fighting. The appointment was for an indefinite period whilst holding that rank, at the end of which time the appointee would revert to his substantive, or definitive rank, against which promotion was based. His appointment was listed in *The London Gazette* of 22 April 1915 (third supplement to the edition of 20 April). In view of his previous military experience it is surprising that Greenwood was not given an immediate commission into an existing battalion and sent to France earlier.

Harry and Helena's second child, a boy, was born on Tuesday 20 July 1915 at their home at Moorlands, Sewardstonebury in Waltham Abbey, near Chingford, Essex. He was named Harry Charles Gillespie - Charles after Harry's father and Gillespie after Helena's father. Tragically the infant died a few days later on 24 July, from complications and "jaundice exhaustion." Harry was given compassionate leave from his battalion to be with Helena, and both birth and death details of their child were registered by Harry on 26 July. Harry junior was buried in Tottenham Cemetery, in what was to become a family plot, near to the chapel.

Mary Ann (Mollie) Greenwood, the youngest daughter of Charles and Margaret, had died in March 1914 and the grave was opened up to provide the final resting place of Harry Charles Gillespie Greenwood. There is a stone cross on three plinths. The front of the cross is inscribed "In the loving memory of" and the front of the plinths record the death of Mollie. On the left side of the plinths is the inscription:

> Also the infant son of
> Harry and Helena
> Greenwood
> who died July 24th 1915
> aged 4 days
> "suffer the little children to come unto me"

A grieving Captain Greenwood returned to his battalion, determined not to let personal tragedy come before duty - as events would soon prove. At the beginning of September 1915 9th KOYLI prepared to leave for France. Leaving England with Greenwood were Lieutenant (later Lieutenant-Colonel) Harold E. Yeo and Lieutenant (later Brigade Major) Lancelot D. Spicer. Thirty-three years later both fellow officers would write obituary tributes to him. After travelling to Folkestone by train the 9th Battalion, led by Lieutenant-Colonel Colmer W. D. Lynch, embarked on the SS *St Seviol* on 11 September. From Boulogne they proceeded to Ostove Rest Camp before being sent to the front. Many in the battalion had no previous experience of war, or had even been abroad before. Greenwood, a veteran of the South African War, knew better than most what to expect but even he had no idea of the horrors of trench warfare awaiting them.

Harry and Helena Greenwood's infant son was buried in the family plot in Tottenham Cemetery, July 1915. (photograph: Derek Hunt)

By the time 9th KOYLI reached France the war was in its fourteenth month and the more experienced battalions of the regiment were already on the Western Front. The 2nd Battalion was among the first troops into France in August 1914 and took part in the retreat from Mons and Le Cateau, where men serving in the battalion won two Victoria Crosses. The 1st Battalion was in the Far East until November 1914. This was not the only battalion which was abroad at the start of the war; in August 1914 half of the British Army was stationed overseas, mainly in India.

Captain Greenwood was soon to see action. Despite earlier British reverses on the Western Front, the Allied Commanders were committed to launch a major campaign in the autumn of 1915. A combined operation was planned in Artois using British and French troops, while the French were to launch a second offensive in Champagne. The Allied assault was due to begin at dawn on 25 September. General Sir Douglas Haig, Commander of the British First Army, was not ready for such a large scale operation but it was forced upon him. To compensate for the lack of men and artillery Haig had insisted on the use of chlorine gas for the opening attack - the first British use of this weapon. At Loos, in France, the gas clouds drifted back over the British lines causing casualties among the first wave of attack troops, and the still intact German machine guns also took their toll.

On the day of the opening attack at Loos, Saturday 25 September 1915, Captain Greenwood had marched with his battalion through the village of Vermelles to reach the British trenches running north east from Loos. The

The Greenwood family 1915.
Back row: (left to right) Arthur, Harry, David. Front row: John, Margaret, Charles.
(photograph: Mrs Patricia Roberts)

Harry Greenwood and his brothers 1915.
Left to right: Harry, Arthur, David, John.

64th Infantry Brigade took part in the attack on the redoubt known as Hill 70 and fierce fighting ensued after the German front line was crossed in the early hours of 26 September. Battalion casualties were two officers wounded and 215 other ranks killed, wounded or missing.

The 9th Battalion War Diaries simply reported that the battalion took part in the attack on Hill 70, returning to the trenches afterwards. This is a surprisingly brief diary note for a new battalion reporting on its first action. Perhaps the reason for this is that 9th KOYLI should not have taken part in the attack. Hill 70 today is just a cross-roads on the busy Lens-Hulluch road but in 1915 was a heavily fortified redoubt.

The War Diaries of 64th Infantry Brigade for 26 September recorded that:

> *At 1.45 pm a renewed attack ... was just being arranged, when the 9th KOYLI were seen moving forward independently. Their CO was at the time at Brigade HQ getting instructions, and had given no orders. It has not yet been discovered who ordered them forward. It was impossible to stop them, and with a few hurried verbal instructions their CO ran off after them. But practically they went off without orders. The 10th KOYLI were hastily ordered to follow in support and their CO was ordered not to go beyond the Loos-Hulluch Road. There was no prospect of two battalions succeeding where many had failed, and it was now hoped merely to restore morale by ending up with an advance of some kind, and then to dig in near the road beyond which further advance seemed impossible.*

But the two battalions and other rallied troops did not halt at the Loos-Hulluch road and pressed on up the slopes of Hill 70. The attack was met with heavy machine-gun fire and the attackers withdrew. The original 64th Infantry Brigade position was held till dusk under heavy bombardment. It was then realised that the men on the hill were British and not German, and the British artillery barrage was lifted.

The War Diaries of 64th Infantry Brigade continued:

> *Only then was it realised that we and our artillery had been assailing our own people in the back most of the day, as a result of imperfect information due probably as far as we were concerned to the fact that we were not intended to share in any attack on Hill 70.*

At midnight the 64th Infantry Brigade was relieved by a Brigade of Guards Division, and on 27 September 9th KOYLI withdrew to bivouac near Vermelles. On 5 October the newly arrived 64th Brigade was inspected by General Sir Herbert Plumer KCB, Commanding Officer Second Army.

The War Diaries do not name the officer responsible for ordering the advance on Hill 70 but it is possible, in view of the rewards he received

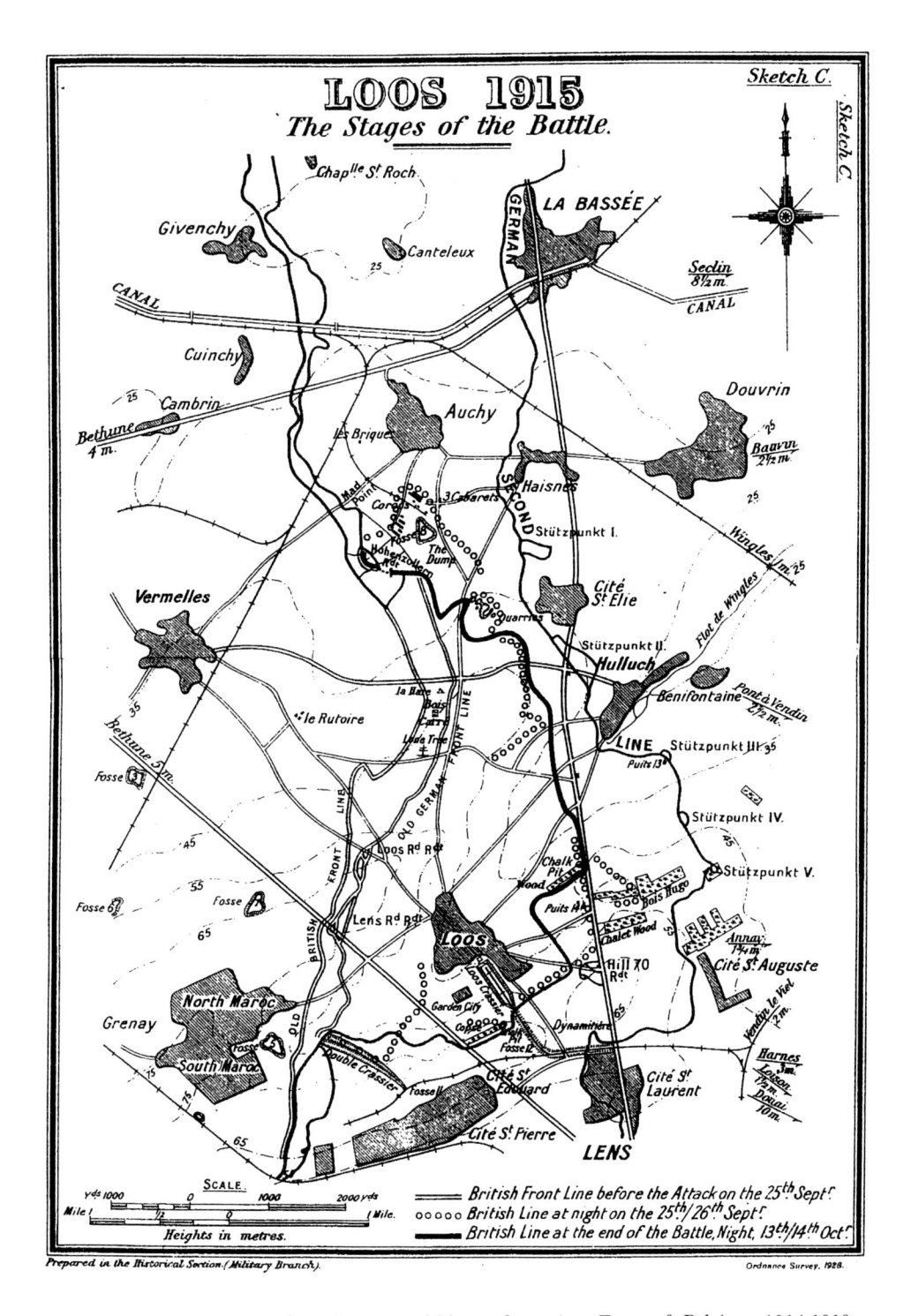

Reproduced from *History of the Great War. Military Operations France & Belgium, 1914-1918*.
Compiled by Brigadier-General Sir James Edmonds.
HMSO 1922-1949.

afterwards, that it may have been Captain Greenwood. He was appointed Temporary Major the following month so he must have impressed his superiors with his leadership skills during the attack, and the Military Cross he received was the most appropriate award in the circumstances.

Because of the manpower and shells shortages the British advances could not be held and the Battle of Loos ended in stalemate. By 16 October, when the battle was effectively over, British losses were over 50,000 men killed. Sir John French was relieved of his command and replaced as Commander-in-Chief of the BEF by General Sir Douglas Haig in December 1915.

King George V visited the front line to review the troops in late October 1915 and Greenwood's battalion was paraded before His Majesty near Bailleul on 28 October. The King was injured when his horse took fright and reared up. He was thrown off and the horse landed on him causing serious injuries including a fractured pelvis.

After the Battle of Loos the composition of 64th Brigade changed and the 1st Battalion East Yorkshire Regiment (1st East Yorkshires) replaced 14th Durham Light Infantry. During October Greenwood and his battalion were in trenches near Ploegsteert, a few miles inside Belgium, moving in November to trenches near Armentieres where they remained for the next few months. On 31 December 1915 he was allowed eight days leave away from the front line and reported for duty on his return on 8 January 1916.

Battalions were regularly rotated within their divisions. The changeovers were carried out mostly after dark to prevent the Germans gaining intelligence about troop movements. It was normal to spend five to seven days in trenches at the front before being relieved by another battalion and retiring to reserve trenches or billets in a nearby town or village. Regular changes were necessary to keep up morale and prevent the troops becoming physically exhausted. But even those areas behind the lines were not safe from enemy shelling. On 15 November 1915 the town of La Tissage was shelled.

The War Diaries of 9th Bn KOYLI recorded:

Fourteen shells landed in and around house occupied as Bn HQ. Three being direct hits. One sentry was killed and eight men wounded.

Several gallantry awards (many without published citations) were made to KOYLI personnel after Loos, and on 14 January 1916 *The London Gazette* announced that Temporary Captain Harry Greenwood had been awarded the Military Cross. There was no citation for this award, but as Hill 70 on Sunday 26 September 1915 was the only action Greenwood had encountered since landing in France it is almost certainly for bravery on that occasion. The Military Cross (MC) was instituted in December 1914 to reward gallantry for junior officers of the rank of Captain and below.

Temporary Captain Greenwood was promoted to Temporary Major on 27 October 1915. The appointment, which was listed in the supplement dated

Hill 70 today. The summit of the redoubt is in the middle of the picture while the cross-roads are on the left.
(photograph: Dorien Clifford)

Hill 70 today, looking about 2k south-east up to the summit from a point about 130 metres in front of the 9th KOYLI position on the Loos-Hulloch Road (not the side road seen on the right of the picture).
(photograph: Dorien Clifford)

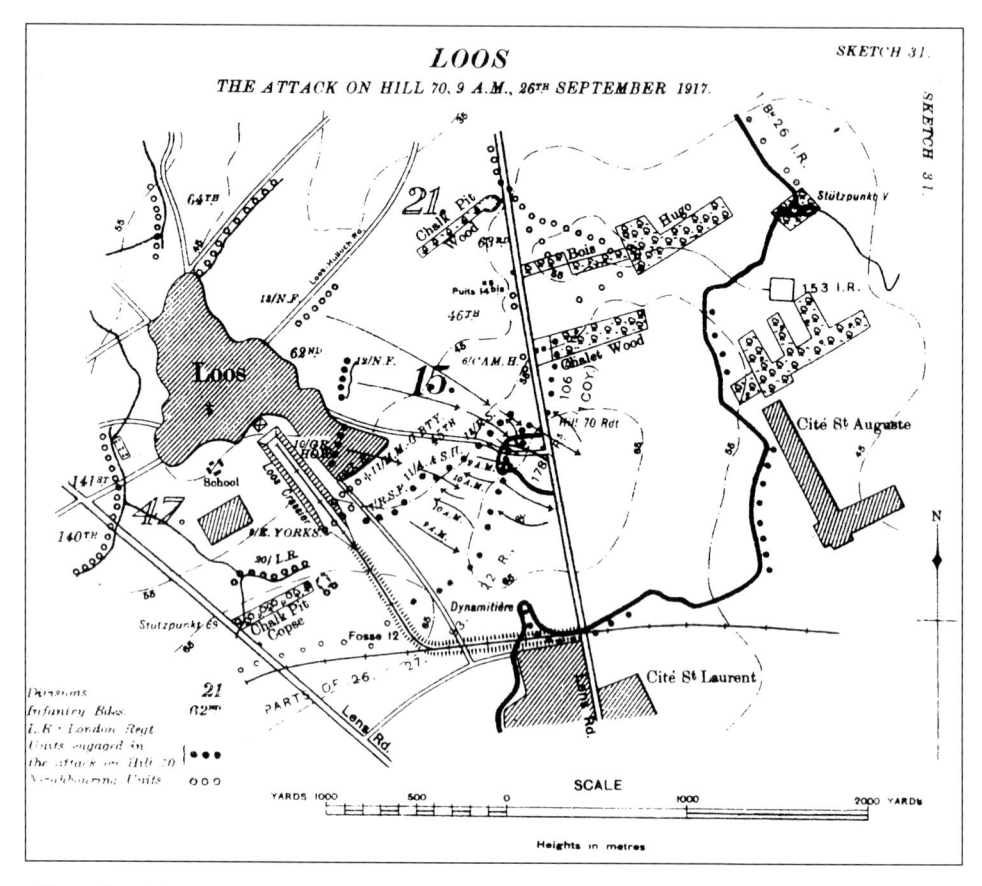

Reproduced from *History of the Great War. Military Operations France & Belgium, 1914-1918.* Compiled by Brigadier-General Sir James Edmonds. HMSO 1922-1949.
(Although the map heading states that the attack on Hill 70 took place at 9.00 am 26 September 1917, it actually took place on the same date in 1915)

18 March to *The London Gazette* of 17 March 1916, was an army rank not a regimental rank. There appears to have been no suitable vacancy for another major in 9th KOYLI at the time. (He was promoted to Temporary Major again in October 1917 - the second time with regimental seniority.)

He was also mentioned in despatches (MID) for the action at Hill 70. Field Marshal French included Captain Greenwood in his list of those recommended "for gallant and distinguished service in the field." The MID was listed in the supplement dated 1 January 1916 to *The London Gazette* of 31 December 1915.

Chapter Four

1916-1917

Loos was to be the last major action for 9th KOYLI until the Battle of the Somme in July 1916. For the next few months the battalion settled down into the now familiar pattern of trench warfare. The winter of 1915/1916 was particularly wet and this is recorded in the Battalion War Diaries (National Archives file WO 95/2162). Comments such as "trenches being pumped continuously" and "water still rising in the trenches" appear all too frequently.

In such conditions trenchfoot, a form of frostbite affecting the feet of soldiers standing for long periods in cold water, was common. Trenchfoot caused numbness and swelling of the feet, and when gangrene set in this usually led to amputation of the affected parts. It would have been of little comfort to know that the Germans were suffering similar conditions. Lice, which carried trench fever, were also a serious problem which the men had to learn to live with as there was not always the opportunity to bathe or change their clothes.

The relative quiet during this period was no doubt due to the enemy being too busy pumping their own trenches to shell British trenches. British and German trenches were separated by a 'no man's land' which varied in depth from a few hundred yards to several miles. This area was usually mined and further protected at each end by lines of barbed wire. Behind the front line were more lines of trenches, linked by communication trenches.

Major Harry Greenwood was temporarily in command of the 9th KOYLI while Lieutenant-Colonel Lynch was away on leave for the period 18 to 31 January 1916. This was a fairly quiet period, with the battalion providing working parties for trench repairs in the Armentieres area.

Meanwhile the rest of the Greenwood family had also answered the call of duty. Harry's father, although over 60, enlisted for war service with the Cheshire Regiment in January 1915. In view of his previous 21 years service with the Grenadier Guards, Charles Greenwood was given immediate promotion to Colour Sergeant (the rank he held when he left the army in 1896). He was transferred to the Territorial Reserve Battalion in 1916 and attached to the Cheshire Volunteer Regiment in April 1917. After a short attachment to the Manchester Regiment he was transferred back to the Cheshire Regiment in January 1918 and finally demobilised in March 1919. He was a Yeoman of the Guard again after demobilisation until his death in 1927.

Harry's brothers had also joined the army, some of them as career soldiers before the war had started. Arthur enlisted in the Royal Artillery

*Charles Greenwood, Harry's father, re-joined the army in January 1915. By 1917 he was acting RSM attached to the Cheshire Volunteer Regiment.
(photograph: Mrs Patricia Roberts)*

in 1906 and served on the North West Frontier in 1908. He was commissioned in 1914 and served in East Africa 1914/15 and later joined the Royal Horse Artillery in France in 1915. After being wounded in 1916 Arthur returned to England and was on Home Service 1917/18 before being transferred to the RAF in 1918.

David enlisted, in 1906, in the Royal Berkshire Regiment before being claimed by his older brother Arthur (in those days an older brother could claim a younger to transfer to his unit). He served in the Royal Artillery in India pre-war, and in France and Mesopotamia during the war. He retired as a battery sergeant-major and after the war joined the Indian Prison Service. John was commissioned in the King's Liverpool Regiment in 1914 and served in France. He was later badly wounded and invalided home.

The four brothers had met up, in uniform, in 1915 for a family photograph. At one point they were all in France at the same time. Remarkably, they all survived the war, although some of them received serious wounds.

Harry's other brother, Charles, had emigrated to Canada in 1907 and joined the Toronto Police. Charles served three years in the army in the Great War, but his regiment was based in Canada. He did not join his brothers on the Western Front, for which Harry never forgave him.

At the time of the family photograph in 1915 Harry and Helena Greenwood were living at Moorlands, Sewardstonebury. Harry wrote frequently to his wife describing life in the trenches, and Helena would write telling how she and Mollie were getting on at home. Unfortunately none of these letters have survived.

9th KOYLI remained in trenches in the Armentieres/Tissage area during January and February 1916. January was relatively quiet but there was more enemy action in February, with the 9th KOYLI trenches suffering frequent shelling and aerial bombing. Snipers were also a constant danger to any man showing his head above the parapet. In March the battalion moved from Armentieres to La Neuville, via Steenwercke where the men stayed in billets.

In February all battalion officers of rank of Captain, with the exception of 'Captain' (T/Major) Greenwood who was an experienced officer by this time, attended a tactical exercise at Divisional HQ. Despite his promotion several months earlier Major Greenwood was frequently referred to as 'Captain' in the Battalion War Diaries during early 1916.

The primitive nature of trench life affected the health of the men who were forced to endure it. In April 1916 Major Greenwood fell ill while with 9th KOYLI near La Neuville, France. He was admitted to a field hospital on 20 April and found to be suffering from epididymitis, a painful swelling of the testes caused by a viral infection, and "general ill-health." His condition was considered serious enough to warrant evacuation to England for treatment and bed rest. He embarked on the SS *St Patrick* at Rouen on 24 April and disembarked at Southampton the following day. After being examined by an Army Medical Board on 2 May he was recommended for six weeks sick leave in the UK. Greenwood did not return from sick leave until 5 July 1916, by which time he had missed the opening stages of the Battle of the Somme.

At 7.30 am on Saturday 1 July 1916 the week-long British barrage of the German lines lifted and the attack began. The start of the bombardment had given the enemy notice of an impending attack, but before the introduction of tank warfare there was no other way of destroying German defensive positions. Taking shelter in their deep undergound dugouts the German Army survived the initial bombardment and emerged at the end of it to set up their machine-gun positions. Over an eighteen mile long line, from Serre in the north to Maricourt in the south, 100,000 British troops left their trenches and walked into no man's land. The previous bombardment had failed to destroy the German lines due to their well constructed trench systems and the poor quality of British shells.

Wave after wave of British troops, almost all volunteers, advanced to be mowed down by machine-guns which they thought had been destroyed. The German machine-gun posts employed Maxim machine-guns, each weighing over 100 lbs. These were mounted on tripods to cover a wide area of fire and had air or water-cooled barrels to prevent overheating. Their rate of fire, 500 rounds per minute, made them lethal against advancing infantry. British soldiers who survived the initial slaughter became entangled on the German barbed wire defences, against which shrapnel shells had proved ineffective.

The new offensive proved to be a tragic miscalculation. There were 57,470 casualties (the equivalent of over 70 9th KOYLI Battalions) on the first day of the Battle - 19,240 of these were killed. This was the worst day for casualties in the history of the British Army.

9th Battalion KOYLI took part in the opening attack near Fricourt and lost 55 officers and men, including the Commanding Officer, Lieutenant-Colonel Lynch. With battalion officers leading their men into battle it is not surprising they suffered the same appalling casualties as other ranks. Greenwood may possibly have owed his life to the debilitating viral infection which, at the time, he was still recovering from.

He reported back for duty on 5 July, but initially did not rejoin 9th KOYLI. On the same day that he returned from sick leave Major Greenwood was posted to the 11th Training Reserve Battalion. He had not fully recovered by then as he was on "light duties only." The following month, on 9 August, he was posted to the 8th Training Reserve Battalion. This battalion, with many others, was stationed at Rugeley Camp in Staffordshire from 16 September onwards, when the camp was set up.

The Training Reserve was established in the summer of 1916 by amalgamating all the existing regimental reserve battalions into one organisation. At that time the old system could not cope with the number of new recruits to be trained. Conscription had been introduced under the Military Services Act 1916, and the new Training Reserve Battalions were better equipped to train the new intakes and to supply new infantry battalions to units overseas. Home leave was more frequent than when

Greenwood was in the trenches on the Western Front, and it was around this period that his daughter Evelyn (born 7 July 1917) was conceived.

Not much is known about Major Greenwood's attachment to the 11th or 8th Training Reserve as the War Diaries of both these battalions appear to have been destroyed. It is known from surviving records at the National Archives that the 8th Battalion was part of the 2nd Training Reserve Brigade (11th Battalion was part of the 3rd Brigade) - each brigade consisting of five battalions consecutively numbered. A breakdown of the Infantry Training Reserve Brigades for October 1916 reveals that 8th Battalion had a staff of 55 officers, 10 warrant officers and 101 sergeants - with a total establishment of 1,299 all ranks. It is also known that a large number of conscientious objectors were sent to Rugeley Camp. Greenwood was later quoted as saying that he had had considerable experience in dealing with them.

Major Greenwood is believed to have been mentioned in despatches (MID) during his time with the Training Reserve Brigade. The Ministry of Defence has a 'possible' MID entry on his personal file for January 1917.

Field Marshal Viscount French, Commander-in-Chief Home Forces, in his despatch of 31 December 1916 paid tribute to the valuable work carried out by the Training Reserve. His despatch, published in *The London Gazette* of 23 January 1917, included the following:

The work of training troops for overseas, both drafts and new units, imposes a great and continuous strain on the Staffs, on the Schools, and on the Reserve Formations. All have responded loyally to the demands made on them, and I consider special credit is due to those officers and NCOs who, with little previous military knowledge, have become most efficient instructors and have thus liberated a great number of officers and NCOs for duty overseas... I desire here to place on record my appreciation of the valuable help in training matters that I have consistently received from the departments of the War Office concerned.

Although this despatch would have been the obvious place for Major Greenwood to be mentioned, his name does not appear to be included in the list of names of those "deserving of special consideration." A search through the indexes of *The London Gazette* has not located the missing MID. It is possible that his name was included in the original despatch (which has since been destroyed) but for some reason it was omitted from *The London Gazette*.

Greenwood's former battalion, 9th KOYLI, remained in the Somme area until 27 September when it was taken out of the line and moved north to the Béthune area. The Battle of the Somme officially ended on 18 November with over a million casualties on both sides. Lieutenant-Colonel C. E. Heathcote had arrived to take command of the battalion in early September, but was admitted to hospital later the same month. His replacement, Lieutenant-Colonel C. A. Milward, was admitted to hospital in January 1917 and was transferred to a posting in India two months later. Lieutenant-Colonel N. R. Daniell assumed command in March 1917.

The battalion spent the first few months of 1917 in re-organisation and training before rejoining 64th Infantry Brigade for a planned new offensive in the Arras area. After the stalemate on the Somme in 1916 a major attack was planned for early 1917. However, before this could be launched the German Army had withdrawn, in February, behind a newly built fortified position - the Hindenburg Line (named after Field Marshal Hindenburg, the German Chief of General Staff).

The Germans left their overstretched front line and destroyed everything they could not take with them. By straightening up their defensive line with purpose-built fortifications they were also able to reduce the number of troops needed to protect it. Another result of the move was the forced postponement of planned Allied attacks. A new British and Canadian offensive in the Arras area was proposed for early April.

The Battle of Arras began on Easter Monday, 9 April 1917. The weather did not favour the attack and a mixture of snow and sleet turned the ground into a quagmire which slowed down advancing troops. Two days earlier 9th and 10th Battalions KOYLI had entered the trenches ready for the attack. 9th Battalion was on the left of the 64th Infantry Brigade, with the 10th Battalion, at first, in brigade reserve. Their objectives were positions on the Hindenburg Line near the Hénin-Héninel road. At the commencement of the attack on the afternoon of 9 April it was discovered that the previous artillery bombardment had failed to completely destroy the enemy wire fences. The delays in trying to find gaps in the wire caused severe casualties to the attackers, and 9th KOYLI took cover in the many shell holes in front of the wire.

The battalion was gradually withdrawn to a point south of Héninel and reinforced by 10th KOYLI. During the night 9th KOYLI was ordered to fall back to a previous objective. Two German counter-attacks on the morning of 10 April were repulsed and the objectives were finally captured. 9th KOYLI casualties in the two days of fighting were three officers and 26 other ranks killed. 64th Infantry Brigade was relieved and moved to Blaireville and then on to Boyelles, south of the River Cojeul.

Major Greenwood returned to 9th KOYLI from the Training Reserve on Tuesday 17 April 1917, just days short of twelve months after leaving France in April 1916. He arrived with a new draft of men from England while the battalion was in training at Blaireville. He was glad to be back in action.

Renewed attacks were made on the Hindenburg Line in early May, but this time 9th and 10th Battalions KOYLI were in the second line of the Brigade. 9th KOYLI moved up to the front line in June, where it remained for the next few months. This must have been a frustrating period for a man of action such as Harry Greenwood, particularly as he had already been out of the fighting for almost a year.

Back in England, Greenwood's second daughter was born in July. Helena Greenwood had temporarily moved out of the Chingford area because of the risk of Zeppelin air raids. These huge hydrogen-filled airships frequently crossed the North Sea to drop bombs on East Anglia, London and the Home Counties before returning to Germany. Helena moved to Devon, where Alice Stella Evelyn was born at 7 Courtland Road, Paignton on Saturday 7 July. The birth was registered by Helena at the end of August 1917.

9th KOYLI spent most of September resting and training in preparation for its part in the Third Battle of Ypres, also known as Passchendaele. The Allied attack began on 31 July and was not progressing as well as expected. Field Marshal Sir Douglas Haig had planned the offensive to remove the Germans from their dominant positions and ultimately capture the Belgian ports used as U-boat bases. Although intended as a strategic breakthrough the determined German defence and the atrocious weather, which transformed the area into a sea of mud, turned the Passchendaele campaign into a war of attrition. Small territorial gains were eventually made, but at considerable cost to both sides. The precise casualty figures will probably never be known but it is estimated that over 60,000 British and Dominion troops died. Thousands of men drowned in the mud.

21st Division took part in an attack in early October, with 64th Infantry Brigade on the right, 62nd on the left and 110th in divisional reserve. 9th and 10th KOYLI moved up into the line on 1 October, the 9th passing through Polygon Wood, east of Ypres, and the 10th held in reserve. On the night of 2/3 October 9th KOYLI moved from a position known as Clapham Junction to relieve the Leicestershire Regiment in trenches at Polygon Wood. They spent the next 24 hours under continuous enemy bombardment and suffered heavy losses.

Battle positions were taken up on the night of 3/4 October for an attack the next day on German positions west of the village of Reutel. This became known as the Battle of Broodseinde. At 6.00 am the attack began and met fierce opposition. Major Greenwood's part in this attack is not recorded but it would have been out of character if he was not taking an active role at the head of the battalion. An enemy barrage descended over the whole area of attack causing serious casualties and cutting off communications. The battalion reached its objective, but during a German bombardment that evening a shell fell on 9th KOYLI HQ mortally wounding the Commanding Officer, Lieutenant-Colonel Daniell. The Commanding Officer of 10th KOYLI temporarily took command of the survivors of both KOYLI battalions.

They continued to move forward, crossing a swamp under machine-gun fire and capturing fortified positions on both sides of the swamp. Their right flank was unprotected and companies from the DLI and East Yorkshires were brought up as reinforcements. The Germans counter-attacked on 5 October but were beaten off. A British barrage descended on the enemy positions and 64th Brigade then advanced under its cover and dug a line of defence. Throughout the next day this line was held against further German counter-attacks. That evening 64th Infantry Brigade was relieved by troops from 7th Division, and 9th KOYLI retired to billets near Zillebeke.

*Men of the KOYLI resting on the way back from the trenches, Wieltje,
1 October 1917. (photograph: Imperial War Museum, Q6026)*

*Men of the KOYLI fusing Stokes Mortar Bombs, near Ypres, 1 October 1917.
(Photograph: Imperial War Museum, Q6454)*

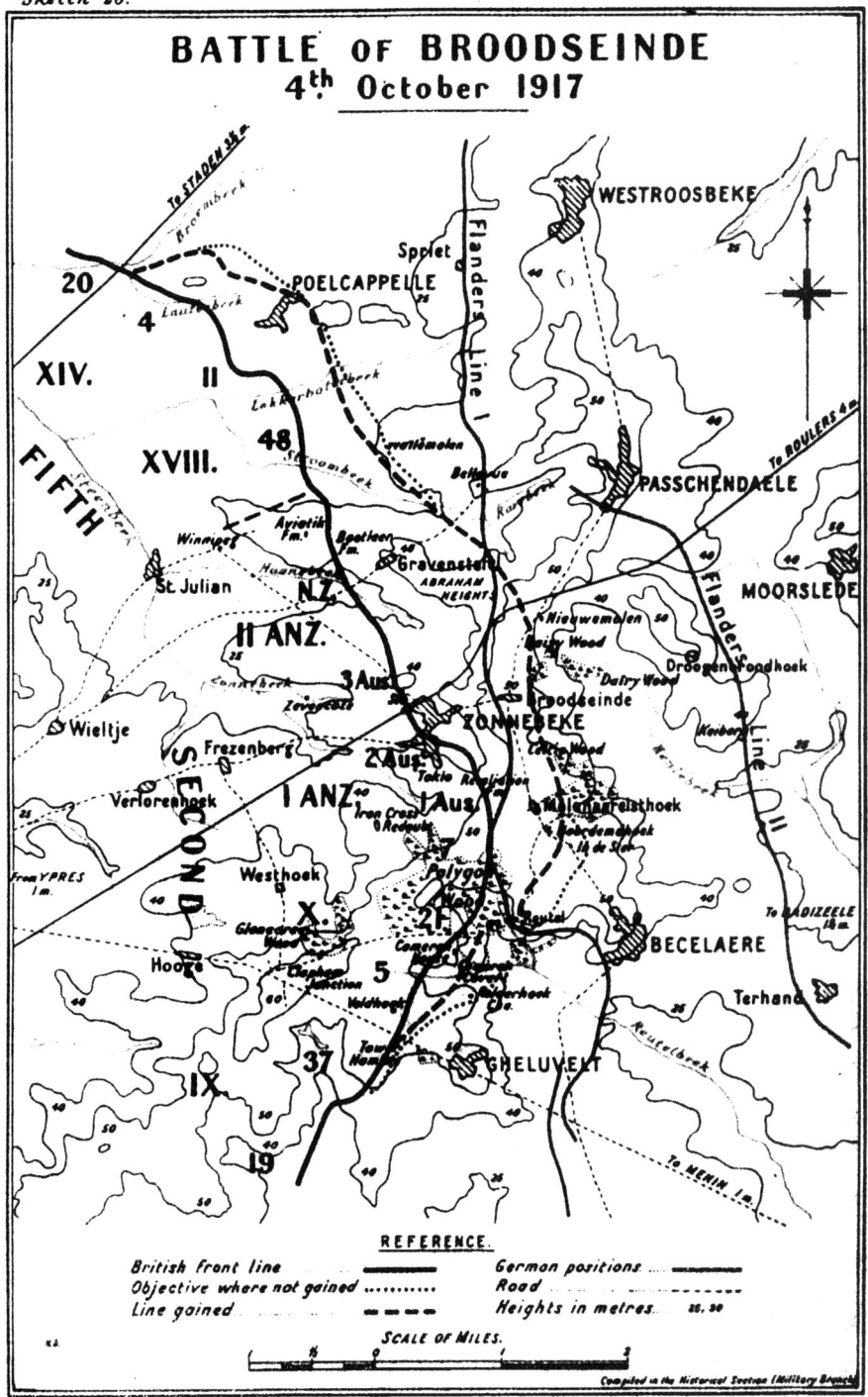

Reproduced from *History of the Great War. Military Operations France & Belgium, 1914-1918.*
Compiled by Brigadier-General Sir James Edmonds. HMSO 1922-1949.

The Regimental History recorded that on Saturday 6 October 1917:

> *The 9th Bn. came out of the trenches 120 strong, including officers. Major H. Greenwood was the senior officer left with the battalion and now commanded it until Lt. Col. A. J. McCulloch took over the command on 10 November.*

Major Greenwood was again promoted to Temporary Major on 19 October, while still temporarily in command of 9th KOYLI. The appointment was listed in the supplement dated 31 January to *The London Gazette* of 29 January 1918. It read:

> *Yorks. Light Infantry*
> *Temp. Major H. Greenwood; from Yorks L. I. (attached) to be temp. Major 19 October 1917, with seniority 27 October 1915, and to be acting Lt. Col. while commanding a Bn. 19 October 1917 to 31 October 1917.*

This second appointment as Major was a regimental promotion and was backdated for seniority for promotion to 27 October 1915, when he received the first appointment. The acting rank of Lieutenant-Colonel only covered the period 9th KOYLI was without a more senior officer and Greenwood reverted to his previous rank afterwards. Interestingly, he appears to have been considered for the acting rank only when he achieved the rank below (i.e. 19 October 1917).

The battalion spent November 1917 resting and refitting near Steenwerck. In December it was sent to the front line near Longavesnes, back in France, where the British trenches were regularly shelled by the Germans. On 31 December 1917 the new Commanding Officer, Lieutenant-Colonel Andrew J. McCulloch, went to a Commanding Officers' course at Divisional HQ and Major Greenwood again assumed command of the battalion.

On the Home Front there had been changes over the past 18 months in the British Government and the Royal Family. Lord Kitchener, who as Secretary for War had done so much to raise the New Armies, was sent to Russia in June 1916 to meet the Tsar. He died when the ship he travelled in, HMS *Hampshire*, was sunk by a mine. Kitchener was succeeded as Secretary for War by David Lloyd George. In December that year Lloyd George became Prime Minister following the resignation of Herbert Asquith, who had been Prime Minister since the beginning of the war.

Conscious of public opinion, King George V had decided in 1917 that it was time for the Royal Family to change its Germanic surname of Saxe-Coburg-Gotha. In its place the King adopted the name Windsor.

Chapter Five

January - May 1918

In early 1918 the number of infantry battalions in a division was reduced from twelve (four battalions to a brigade - three brigades to a division) to nine. This was made necessary by a reduction in the number of new recruits arriving from the UK to replace casualties. Lloyd George lacked faith in Field Marshal Haig and deliberately cut back on the reinforcements asked for. He felt this would prevent Haig mounting another offensive as costly in British lives as Passchendaele. Many battalions were broken up, usually those which had suffered the greatest losses and whose ranks were most difficult to fill. As a result of these changes 10th KOYLI was incorporated into the 9th Battalion and twelve officers and 250 other ranks were transferred from 10th to 9th KOYLI.

Major Greenwood was temporarily in command of 9th KOYLI in January 1918 while the battalion was near Epéhy in the front line and Lieutenant-Colonel McCulloch was in command of 64th Infantry Brigade. Greenwood was an experienced officer and had deputised for the commanding officer on other occasions.

He had previously held the acting rank of Lieutenant-Colonel for the period 19 to 31 October 1917 while commanding 9th KOYLI, and this acting appointment was gazetted on 31 January 1918.

In February 9th KOYLI was again in the front line before returning to the divisional reserve at Haut Allaines. The first few months of the year were to be one of the quietest periods of the war and the battalion spent much of the time carrying out essential repairs to its trenches and the construction of a third line of defences, often in appalling weather.

The Battalion War Diaries reported in January:

The trenches were practically untenable owing to the thaw ... Enemy very quiet and apparently in as much trouble over the trenches as we are as he allowed our men to expose themselves without shooting at them.

However, this relative peace was soon to be shattered as General Erich Ludendorff, the German Chief-of-Staff, was planning a major offensive in the Somme area near St Quentin. For over three years the Germans had been content merely to defend the territory they gained in the first few months of the war. But circumstances had now changed.

Russia had withdrawn from the war after the 1917 Bolshevik Revolution and Germany was able, during early 1918, to transfer its eastern armies to the Western Front. Another factor in the timing of the German Spring Offensive was America's decision to enter the war. The German High Command knew that any new offensive would have to be started before American troops could be brought to the front in sufficient numbers to tip the balance in favour of the Allies.

When the German attack, codenamed 'Operation Michael', began on the morning of Thursday 21 March Major Greenwood and 9th KOYLI were in the Brown Line (the second line of defence trenches) near Guyencourt. 21st Division was then part of the Fifth Army. This part of the front was over-extended, with too few men to defend the part of the line which bore the brunt of the attack. An enemy offensive had been expected and some German prisoners had even disclosed the correct date, but it was not known where the attack would take place.

9th KOYLI was ordered, in the early afternoon, to leave its positions to occupy trenches south of Guyencourt and to maintain observation posts only on the Brown Line. The Battalion War Diaries reported that "The bombardment was now steady, though hardly intense, enemy's shells bursting every half minute." Orders were received at 4.40 pm to return to the Brown Line. 15th DLI was already there and they were later joined by 1st East Yorkshires, making up the rest of 64th Brigade. These British trenches were subjected to continuous enemy shelling, although the main bombardment was directed at the front line. 15th DLI later recaptured sections of the Yellow Line (rear line) which had been overrun.

The German bombardment continued the next day. On the afternoon of 22 March it was reported that the Germans were advancing in force from the direction of Peiziers, on the right flank of the brigade which was particularly vulnerable. Under cover of mist the enemy had captured Epéhy and were attacking the front line positions. Orders were received from Divisional HQ that a withdrawal to the Green Line, the next line of defence, was to take place at 7.30 that evening. Shortly after receipt of these orders, however, the Germans broke through the defences and practically surrounded the 1st East Yorkshires holding the right flank near Villers Faucon. A running battle developed through Saulcourt between two German battalions and the East Yorkshires. The forced withdrawal of this battalion exposed the right flank of 9th KOYLI to enemy machine-gun fire. After a fierce fight, and a withdrawal across the valley where the enemy barrage went down, Major Greenwood and his battalion were able to make their way to the Green Line, arriving there at around 8.00 pm.

Five officers and 70 other ranks had been killed or wounded in the withdrawal. Many were listed as missing and only 16 officers and 160 other ranks were present at the new rendezvous.

The German onslaught continued and on 23 March orders were received to withdraw from the Green Line to a line between Aizecourt le Haut and Bussu. Earlier that day the enemy made two strong attacks on the positions held by 9th KOYLI. Both attacks were repulsed. The first attack was launched at 6.30 am during a thick mist and the Germans came to within 30 yards of the 9th KOYLI defences before being driven back.

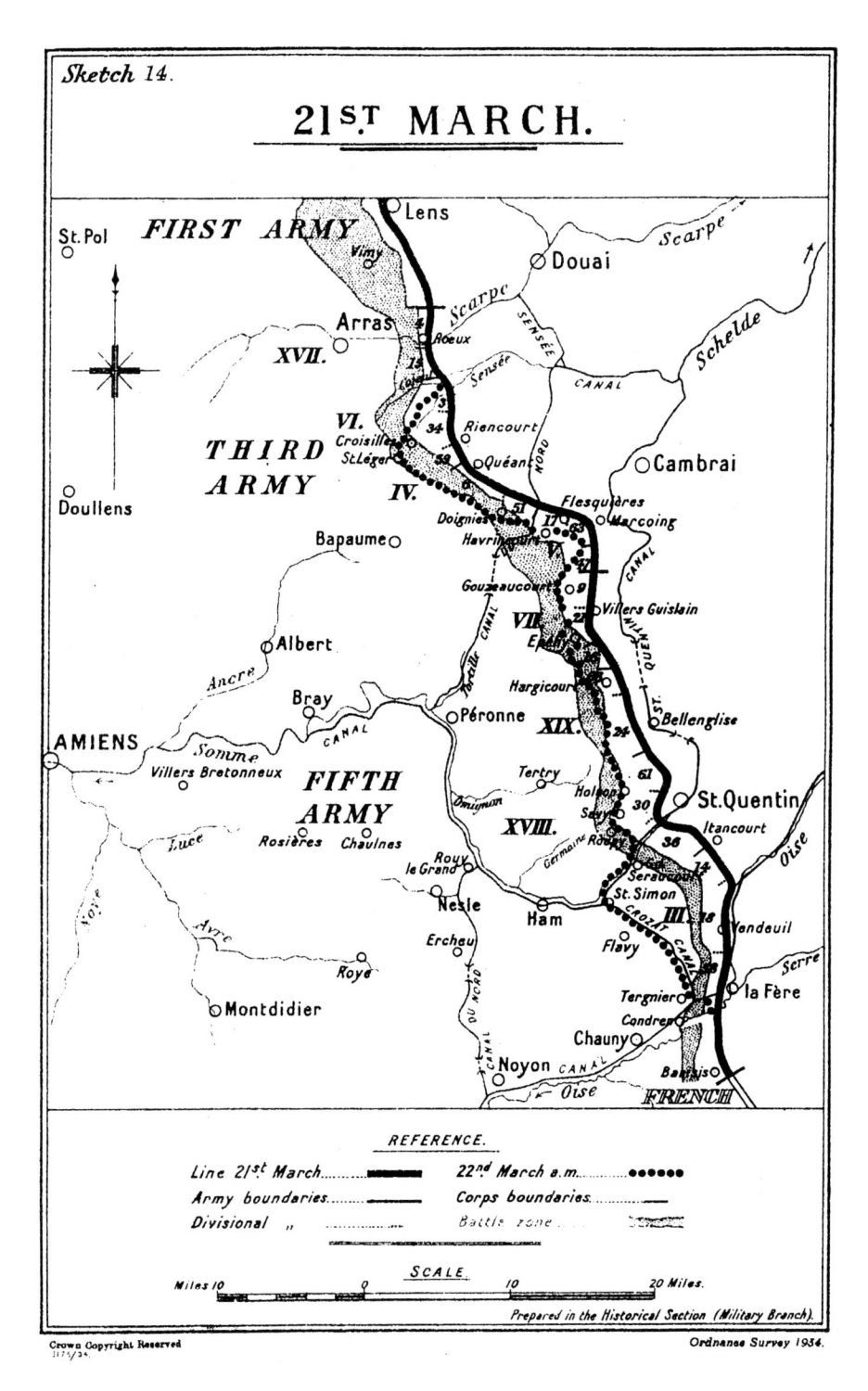

Reproduced from *History of the Great War. Military Operations France & Belgium, 1914-1918.*
Compiled by Brigadier-General Sir James Edmonds. HMSO 1922-1949.

Enemy artillery appeared to be poorly co-ordinated as shells flew directly over the British positions without inflicting casualties.

The Regimental History of KOYLI reported that:

> *At 7.30 am a second attack was delivered, still under cover of the mist. This time the fire of the defenders was withheld until the last moment and many Germans dropped right in front of the wire. Again the attack was broken up. Major H. Greenwood with no. 38787 Pte H. Wright and a Lance-Corporal of the 1st East Yorkshire Regiment, taking advantage of the mist, immediately rushed out to the place where the wire joined the Longavesnes-Péronne road in order to secure two German machine-guns which were lying on the road, and to use them on the retiring enemy. He encountered a heap of dead Germans and an officer and two unwounded soldiers who held up their hands; although unarmed, Major Greenwood secured the prisoners, who were marched in.*
> *They belonged to the 221st (German) Machine Gun Company: the officer said that in civil life he was a professor of philosophy. The Adjutant, Captain Hendriks, who had just been wounded, conducted the prisoners to the division. This action on the part of Major Greenwood raised the spirits of the men, so much so that, when at 9.00 pm an order was received for a retirement from the position, the idea of retirement was most unpopular; it was hard in the fog to understand the necessity for a move which was becoming vitally urgent owing to the falling back of the main line.*

Although the German officer and his men quickly surrendered when they saw Major Greenwood approaching, they just as quickly changed their minds when they realised he was alone and unarmed. The sudden arrival of Private Wright and the Lance-Corporal, both carrying rifles, persuaded the Germans to surrender once more.

The War Diaries of 64th Infantry Brigade noted the significant part played by 9th KOYLI that day:

> *Four light MGs, an officer and a few prisoners, were captured. The machine-guns were then used most successfully against the Germans and inflicted many casualties.*

The withdrawal to the south of Aizecourt le Haut was completed, but with serious losses for the battalion, as the Germans had by then breached the left flank. Eight officers and 100 other ranks were killed or wounded. The enemy also suffered serious losses and it was estimated that 250 Germans died in the attack on Guyencourt.

Further enemy advances made the new position insecure and later on 23 March a withdrawal was made to a point near Cléry, a few miles west of Péronne. The Germans attacked again the following day and captured

Cléry. 9th KOYLI (by now about 40 men strong) helped in checking the German advance to the north of Brigade HQ and three times repulsed the enemy. The scattered remains of 64th Brigade were ordered to withdraw to Suzanne, on the north bank of the River Somme, reaching the new position late in the evening. The War Diaries of 64th Brigade noted that "the general spirit and morale of the survivors remained high."

On 25 March 9th KOYLI moved to Bray, in the Somme area, and on 26 March Lieutenant-Colonel McCulloch took command of what remained of all the battalions of 21st Division (approximately 1,200 men) to defend a line from the River Somme to the Bray-Corbie road. This composite force defended the line until dusk and then moved back to Mericourt. The Germans did not attack as expected, but were seen to be digging in.

Fortunately by then the German offensive had run out of momentum. Towards the end of the month the enemy started consolidating the positions they had already seized. This gave the British Army much needed time to re-organise and 9th KOYLI resumed its battalion formation on 31 March. Since 21 March, when the German offensive had begun, 64th Infantry Brigade had lost 56 officers (out of a total of just over 60) and almost 1,200 other ranks. With the stalemate of trench warfare ended and the war mobile again, 1918 was to be the most active year of the war for the brigade.

Ludendorff launched a second offensive, 'Operation Georgette', north of Béthune in April and again his armies made rapid territorial gains. However, his desperately needed breakthrough was never achieved and the Germans discontinued the offensive, known as the Battle of the Lys, at the end of April 1918.

At the beginning of the month 9th KOYLI, then part of the Second Army, had moved to Amiens and then to a position south east of Ypres, Belgium. The battalion consisted mainly of new recruits and was initially held back from the German assault, which began on Tuesday 9 April. But the Germans were making such rapid advances during the early part of 'Georgette' that all battalions of the 64th Infantry Brigade were urgently required. By 20 April 9th KOYLI was back in action in the trenches in Onraet Wood, where it relieved units of 15th DLI and 1st East Yorkshires. After being subjected to enemy shelling 9th KOYLI was relieved on 23 April but was back in the trenches two days later.

On Thursday 25 April a German gas attack, from which most of the officers and many men of 9th KOYLI suffered effects, was followed up by an enemy attack. As the Battalion War Diaries recorded: "The battalion got into position and, as the Germans advanced, dealt out death with such success that the German attack came to a standstill." During the battle the Commanding Officer, Lieutenant-Colonel McCulloch, was wounded in the face by a German sniper. Although in pain he carried on, and early the next morning led his battalion in a counter-attack.

As 9th KOYLI advanced at 4.25 am it was noticed that the units providing left and right flanks were not moving forward as planned. Enemy machine-gun fire was then concentrated on the solitary battalion

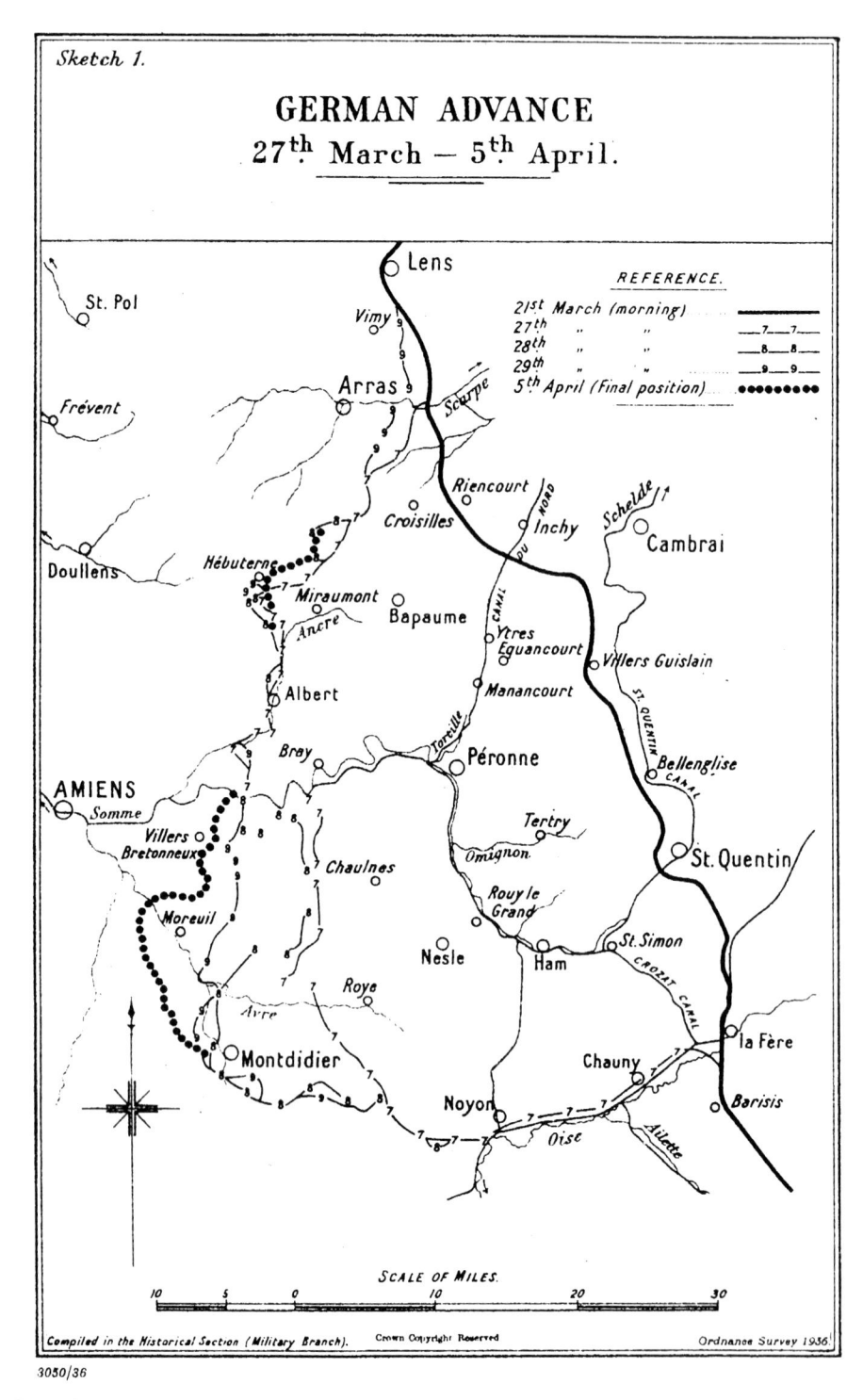

Reproduced from *History of the Great War. Military Operations France & Belgium, 1914-1918.*
Compiled by Brigadier-General Sir James Edmonds. HMSO 1922-1949.

advancing and 9th KOYLI received serious casualties. The attack had to be abandoned when both supporting flanks were held up by heavy machine-gun fire and a promised barrage did not materialise. A further withdrawal was necessary and the battalion, now in new trenches, was subjected to a three hour enemy barrage. Later that day Lieutenant-Colonel McCulloch went back to the field hospital to have his wound dressed. By then his face was very painful and he was also suffering respiratory problems caused by the gas he had inhaled. Major Greenwood took command of the depleted battalion, numbering approximately 100 men, in his absence.

In the evening of 26 April orders were received arranging for the relief of 64th Brigade. This was completed in the early hours of 28 April under cover of darkness and mist, and 9th KOYLI marched back to Red Horseshoe Camp at Reninghelst. The following day the battalion marched to Steenvoorde, where it bivouaced for the night in a field, then marched to Lederzeele.

On 29 April news was received of several gallantry awards, including the Distinguished Service Order (DSO) for Lieutenant-Colonel McCulloch and Major Greenwood. The DSO for Greenwood was for the capture of the machine-guns and prisoners on the Longavesnes-Péronne road on 23 March, thirty months after his first gallantry award (MC) in September 1915. This was formally announced in *The London Gazette* of 26 July 1918. Greenwood would have been delighted to note that Private Harold Wright received the Military Medal for his part in the same action. Wright's award was gazetted on 16 July 1918.

In the absence of the Commanding Officer, who was still on sick leave, Major Greenwood presented medal ribbons to 14 men in the battalion who had been awarded the Military Medal (MM). The medal, which had been introduced in March 1916, was awarded to NCOs and men for acts of bravery and was inscribed "FOR BRAVERY IN THE FIELD." The presentations took place on 3 May while the battalion was resting and rekitting at Lederzeele. Private Wright was one of the men who proudly received his MM ribbon.

Being a determined fighter himself Harry Greenwood could appreciate that quality in others. In a rare speaking engagement after the war he recalled the story of an officer under his command who was out of favour with HQ. When asked for his opinion of the officer he replied "Well, Sir, he'll fight anybody at any time in any place and in any fashion, and he's good enough for me!"

Orders were received for the battalion to proceed to St Omer railway station for transportation to the south, and on 4 May 9th KOYLI began a two day train journey to the Champagne region. After a stop at Pontoise, near Paris, for breakfast on 5 May everyone was delighted to be travelling in green and fertile country, untouched by war. The journey ended at Bouleuse and the battalion marched to Romigny where it stayed "in a splendid French camp, all officers and men having beds" (War Diaries). After resting and training for a week 9th KOYLI marched northwards towards the River Aisne and on 21 May relieved the 15th DLI in the forward trenches. Lieutenant-Colonel McCulloch had rejoined his battalion from sick leave on 17 May. During this period 21st Division was one of several 'tired' British divisions attached to the French Sixth Army so that fresh French troops could be sent to active British fronts.

The Champagne producing region of France was centred around Reims (Rheims), an historic city with a 14th century cathedral. This area had not seen much action recently and was considered "a quiet front." 9th KOYLI and the rest of the division were sent to the area between Soissons and Reims to recuperate after the fierce fighting seen in the past few months. Ironically, this normally quiet area was soon to become very active.

On Monday 27 May the German Army launched its third major Spring Offensive, this time in the Reims area of the River Aisne. As before the Germans made good initial gains, but were held by determined Allied resistance, including newly arrived American divisions.

A huge German bombardment and gas attack starting at 1.00 am, followed by an infantry advance, marked the opening of this latest offensive. In the sector held by 9th KOYLI the trenches were overrun despite determined resistance by the defenders and the battalion suffered heavy losses as it was pushed back. Battalion HQ was attacked late morning by German grenadiers and forced to withdraw to a safer position. The battle raged all day and the enemy, never more than 40 yards away, were kept at bay overnight. Fighting recommenced at dawn on 28 May at the battalion's new position south of Cauroy and it soon became necessary to take up new positions along the Trigny heights. Enemy grenade and rifle attacks were held off all day, but at about 6.00 am Lieutenant-Colonel McCulloch received gunshot wounds to his side. Having not long returned to duty after his previous wounds he was reluctant to report sick, but he later went to the dressing station and handed over temporary control of the battalion, once more, to Major Greenwood.

Further German advances made it necessary for the battalion to fall back again on 29 May. At 3.00 that morning 9th KOYLI abandoned the Trigny heights and joined the remainder of the brigade on the other side of the River Vesle. Bridges over the river were destroyed and a new position established. At 1.00 am on 30 May French reinforcements arrived and 64th Brigade was relieved and moved approximately seven miles south to Marfaux. On 31 May 9th KOYLI moved to Chaltrait where the men were able to rest and the battalion was able to make its numbers up.

The Battle of the Aisne lasted until 6 June. Although the German Army had created a salient in that sector it proved too narrow to defend. General Ludendorff had failed to hold on to any of his objectives and his armies were forced to retreat, which badly affected their morale. For his part in this action Lieutenant-Colonel McCulloch was awarded a bar to his DSO.

There were three main German offensives during the spring of 1918. Ultimately they achieved very little for the German Army, but they did cause considerable casualties on both sides. 9th KOYLI suffered as much as any other unit and at one point in March was reduced to 40 men. Fortunately the next few months would prove less demanding for the battalion and allow it to reinforce its numbers.

Chapter Six

June - October 1918

June was a comparatively quiet month for 9th KOYLI, now back in the British sector. The battalion was at Congy at the beginning of the month before moving to Beacham Le Vieux on 18 June, where the men were billeted in the town after receiving a reception from the Mayor. The Battalion War Diaries recorded the following news:

> *5 June   The Brigadier having gone on leave to England, Major H. Greenwood DSO. MC. took over the command of the Brigade.*
>
> *8 June   Lt. Col. A. J. McCulloch DSO. DCM. having recovered from his wound returned to the battalion and relieved Major H. Greenwood DSO. MC. of the temporary command of the Brigade.*

Although not yet a battalion commander Major Greenwood clearly had the confidence of his superiors to hold such a senior rank, even temporarily.

Re-organisation and amalgamation of British battalions continued and on 24 June 9th KOYLI received the shock news that it was to be reduced to the status of a cadre battalion. (Cadre in military terms is the nucleus of trained professional servicemen forming the basis for the training of new units.) The battalion was no longer required as a fighting unit - it was to leave the brigade and the great majority of its officers and men were to be transferred to other battalions.

Brigadier-General H. R. Headlam, Commanding 64th Infantry Brigade, wrote of his "very deep regret - a regret shared by all ranks in the Brigade - at the departure of this fine battalion." In a Special Brigade Order to all ranks he added that:

> *Since its formation in 1914 the battalion has served continuously with the 64th Brigade and has taken a leading and very distinguished part in all the actions in which the Brigade has taken part. At Loos, on the Somme in 1916, at Arras and Ypres in 1917, and in the three great German offensives on the Somme, round Ypres and in Champagne in 1918, as well as in continuous trench warfare the battalion always upheld the name of the distinguished regiment to which it belongs and its work cannot fail to fill a glorious page in the chronicles of the regiment when the history of its share in this Great War is written.*

Lists were drawn up of the officers and men to remain in the 9th (Cadre) Battalion. Because of his previous experience in the Training Reserve, Major Greenwood was the natural choice to stay on as the Commanding Officer of the new battalion. Fortunately the decision to downgrade 9th KOYLI was reconsidered before the transfers could be carried out and the battalion survived as a full fighting unit for the remainder of the war.

Major Greenwood travelled to England in July for the investiture of his DSO. He received his award from HM King George V at an investiture ceremony at Buckingham Palace on Wednesday 10 July. This was one of those rare occasions where the award was made before being promulgated in *The London Gazette* (Gazetted over two weeks later on 26 July). At the same ceremony Private Henry Nicholas, 1st Battalion Canterbury Infantry, New Zealand Expeditionary Force, received the Victoria Cross.

Greenwood's wife Helena and their eldest daughter Mollie accompanied him to the Palace. His sister Kitty (Kate) was also invited. The picture of the family holding hands while leaving the Palace is often mistakenly said to be of the VC investiture. It shows the extremes of clothing worn to cope with the British weather. The policeman standing next to the Palace gates was equipped with a raincape while Mollie Greenwood, aged four, wore a summer dress. Met Office records show that the day started off with showers but was generally dry in the afternoon when the family left the Palace. It is most likely that Harry's youngest daughter Cynthia (born 1 April 1919) was conceived while he was home on this leave.

Harry Greenwood leaving Buckingham Palace after receiving his DSO 10 July 1918. Left to right: Kitty (sister), Mollie, Harry, Helena.

The Distinguished Service Order (DSO) citation published in the fifth supplement dated 26 July to *The London Gazette* of 23 July 1918, read:

For conspicuous gallantry and devotion to duty during two heavy attacks, made under cover of mist. They were repulsed, but a hostile machine-gun detachment, which succeeded in getting within 50 yards of the line, suffered severely, and an officer and two men ran back to cover. The battalion being very short of machine-gunners owing to casualties, he, with a N.C.O., rushed out with the greatest daring, found the officer and men hiding in a hollow with a heavy machine-gun, and made them carry it back, being all the time under intense fire. The gun was used later on the enemy with great effect.

While Greenwood was in England to receive his DSO, 9th KOYLI was training at Puchevillers and later in the month in brigade reserve at Mailly Maillet. July was a quiet month for the battalion, and deservedly so after the hard fighting of earlier months. Mailly Maillet was occasionally shelled by the Germans, sometimes causing casualties, but there was no real action during this period.

On 25 July Lieutenant-Colonel McCulloch was appointed Officer-in-Charge of the Divisional School for Company Commanders at Acheux. Until a replacement was found, Major Greenwood was temporarily in command of 9th KOYLI. Brigadier-General Headlam was appointed Inspector of Training on 27 July and that day paid a farewell visit to all the battalions in his Brigade. Lieutenant-Colonel McCulloch succeeded him as Brigade Commander of 64th Infantry Brigade - his second appointment in less than a week.

The following day Greenwood replaced McCulloch as Commanding Officer of 9th KOYLI, a role in which he was already very experienced, with the Acting rank of Lieutenant-Colonel. His promotion, effective from 12 August, was listed in a supplement dated 21 September to *The London Gazette* of 20 September 1918.

Brigadier-General Andrew Jameson McCulloch DSO, DCM, BA, was the son of Lord Ardwell, a Scottish Judge, and Lady Ardwell and had been educated at Edinburgh Academy, St Andrew's University and New College, Oxford. He was a career officer and had served with the Highland Light Infantry and the 7th Dragoon Guards before being appointed Commanding Officer of 9th KOYLI in November 1917. During the War he was mentioned in despatches three times and wounded three times.

Greenwood and McCulloch greatly respected each other; they both led from the front and inspired loyalty in others. But this new working relationship between 9th KOYLI and 64th Infantry Brigade was not to last for long. Brigadier-General McCulloch was wounded while leading an attack in Battery Valley on 24 August, the same day that Greenwood was injured by 'friendly fire', and did not return to command the brigade afterwards.

Many of the new soldiers sent to replace 9th KOYLI casualties were 18 year olds and to them their Commanding Officer was a father figure.

Lieutenant-Colonel Greenwood could arouse tremendous loyalty and devotion through example and leading his men into battle rather than sending them off. He could also command great trust as he would never expect his men to do anything he would not do himself, no matter how dangerous. In the battles ahead they would see him personally lead daring attacks, repel counter-attacks and charge enemy machine-gun posts single-handed.

The battalion was back in action again in August, near Albert on the Somme. On 8 August British, Australian and Canadian divisions launched a surprise attack on the German trenches east of Amiens. This was to be the start of the German collapse and the Allies soon captured many of the Somme battlefields they had failed to hold onto two years earlier. General Ludendorff described 8 August as "the black day of the German Army in the history of this war."

Following the attack on their lines the Germans carried out some retaliatory shelling along the brigade front, and 9th KOYLI suffered more casualties. Two days later the battalion was in reserve, then on 14 August back at the front at Beaumont Hamel. On 15 August 9th KOYLI tested the enemy position ahead of it and was met with heavy gun fire, but not before it had destroyed two machine-gun posts. The battalion returned to reserve again on 16 August.

Greenwood often made lone reconnaissance trips across British lines into no man's land at night and on more than one occasion was shot at by his own men while coming back. One night a nervous young sentry took several shots at him, missing each time. He is said to have tapped the soldier on the shoulder with his swagger stick and sternly informed him: "You will have to learn to shoot better than that, young man, if you want to stay in my battalion."

After several days spent refitting and training the battalion moved forward to a point on the Brown Line around midnight 20/21 August, and the next morning moved to a reserve position on the Beaussart-Puisieux road. Following considerable enemy shelling, which caused many casualties, the battalion was ordered to the rear of Battery Valley. 21st Division (V Corps, Third Army) took part in the new Amiens Offensive. There was no preliminary bombardment of the enemy positions as the Allied Armies were using a large number of tanks.

On 22 August 9th KOYLI received orders for a night attack on the other side of the River Ancre. (Bridgeheads were to be established by other battalions.) Their trenches were heavily shelled at dawn and intermittent shelling continued all day. The next day the battalion made its way to Logger Lane, to the south of the Ancre near St Pierre-Division, to form up with the rest of 64th Infantry Brigade. The 1st East Yorkshires were on the left flank and 9th KOYLI on the right flank, both battalions leaving one company in reserve. Also held in reserve was the 15th DLI. A supporting British barrage started at 11.15 pm, and at 11.30 pm the first wave of attackers moved forward in an easterly direction. Lieutenant-Colonel Greenwood personally led his battalion.

Sketch 14

OPERATIONS OF THE THIRD AND FIRST ARMIES

Reproduced from *History of the Great War. Military Operations France & Belgium, 1914-1918.*
Compiled by Brigadier-General Sir James Edmonds.
HMSO 1922-1949.

Logger Lane today. The area where 9th KOYLI assembled before the attack in August 1918. The turning on the left of the picture crosses the River Ancre approximately 500 metres further on and the road ahead leads to Grandcourt.
(photograph: Dorien Clifford)

Logger Lane today. The Grandcourt-Thiepval road, which 9th KOYLI crossed from left to right.
(photograph: Dorien Clifford)

Strongly held German machine-gun positions were soon cleared, in the darkness, and prisoners and enemy machine-guns captured. Further enemy positions were taken in the early hours of 24 August when the battalion reached Battery Valley, which was to the west of the Grandcourt road.

The Battalion War Diaries summed up the situation on Saturday 24 August:

Continuing under heavy machine-gun fire the battalion advanced towards the objective - the Red Line on the Grandcourt-Thiepval road. Before arriving there several shells from our heavy batteries fell short causing some casualties amongst our men; Lt. Col. Greenwood being blown violently off his feet and thrown against a post injuring him internally. In spite of this he continued to lead the battalion towards the objective.

Brigadier-General McCulloch, CO 64th Infantry Brigade, who was also wounded that day, wrote in the Brigade's War Diaries:

On descending into the Battery Valley (time 12.00 midnight) five short bursts from our own artillery fell on our front line and caused about 30 casualties. I understand those bursts were not Divisional but Corps heavy artillery. This mistake was inexcusable as the barrage was timed to lift from Newcomers Lane at 11.45 according to previous arrangements.

In times of stress the human body releases adrenaline, a hormone, into the bloodstream thereby increasing heart and pulse rates and raising blood levels of glucose. Surges of adrenaline have often been credited with enabling wounded soldiers to ignore their wounds and continue fighting. So it was with Lieutenant-Colonel Greenwood. He was obviously more seriously injured than he was prepared to admit to himself or his men, but not bothering about his injuries he pushed himself forward and continued the attack.

Having reached the Grandcourt road (Red Line) 9th KOYLI proceeded to dig in, about 400 yards ahead of the objective. Its right flank was exposed, however, as 110th Brigade had not arrived to protect this side. 15th DLI was brought forward from reserve to fill the gap.

A further advance was made around 3.00 am on 24 August, with less than two hours before daylight. The next objective in Boom Ravine was soon reached but 9th KOYLI, on the left of the attack, was in a highly exposed position without support on either side. In the moonlight the Germans fired at them from all sides. Undaunted, 9th KOYLI charged and captured machine-gun positions on both flanks and in front of them. It was about 4.30 am when the battalion reached its next objective in Boom Ravine and dug in, occupying lines of shell holes. 15th DLI had arrived shortly afterwards, although contact was lost with the 1st East Yorkshires.

Battery Valley area today, seen from the Grandcourt-Thiepval road.
(photograph: Dorien Clifford)

Battery Valley today, seen from further north-east along the same road.
(photograph: Dorien Clifford)

BATTERY VALLEY and BOOM RAVINE, Somme Region 23/24 August 1918.
Arrows show direction of British attack

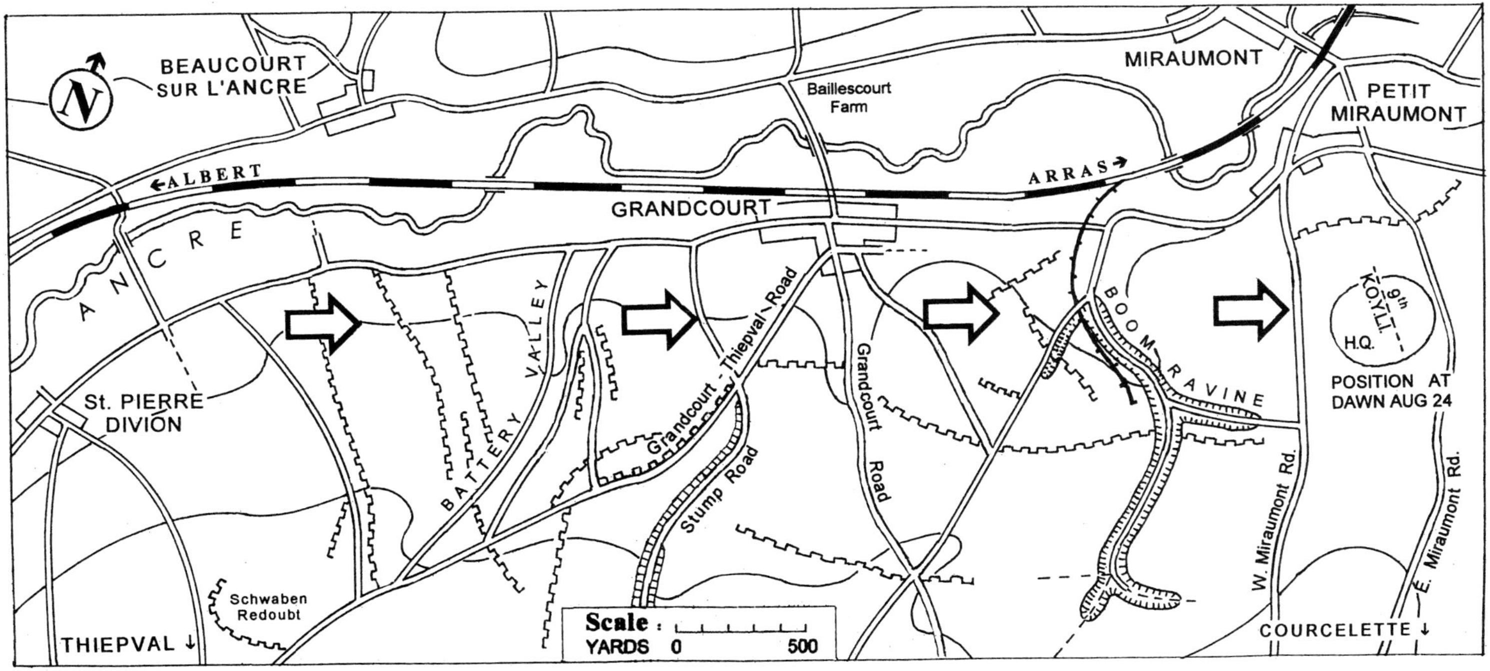

Map by Dorien Clifford

Brigadier-General McCulloch, who was leading his brigade's attack, was wounded and the Commanding Officer of 15th DLI temporarily took command of 64th Brigade. Lieutenant-Colonel Greenwood may well have taken command of the brigade himself had he not already been wounded and still in some pain.

For his "conspicuous gallantry and ability to command" Brigadier-General McCulloch was awarded a second bar to his DSO. The citation recorded that "the advance was over the worst country, and the right flank of the brigade was entirely uncovered throughout. Success was entirely due to his magnificent leadership, moving at the head of this brigade."

When daylight broke it was discovered that the remains of the two battalions were surrounded. The Germans had counter attacked from the unprotected right flank and re-occupied an area Greenwood and the leading battalions of the brigade had already passed, threatening to cut them off from the rest of 21st Division. Despite being outnumbered and ignoring frequent calls to surrender a gallant stand was made.

After Brigadier-General McCulloch had been wounded Captain Spicer, the Brigade Major, carried on the re-organisation of the brigade and consolidation of the position. He was awarded the DSO for his part in this action. The citation recorded that "his arrangements were very instrumental in causing the defeat of repeated counter-attacks. Later when the force was entirely surrounded, he crawled out and brought back a report of the situation which enabled arrangements to be made for the relief of the Brigade."

9th KOYLI casualties were high, but they fought off repeated enemy attacks. Greenwood, still suffering from the wounds he received earlier in the day, continued to inspire his men to perform seemingly impossible tasks. The Germans (units from the 16th Reserve Division) eventually retreated at mid-day having suffered severe losses; some 130 of their dead were later discovered in front of the 9th KOYLI lines. Relief troops advanced on both flanks and the survivors of the siege were rescued. By 7.00 pm that evening the 64th Infantry Brigade was withdrawn to divisional reserve and 9th KOYLI spent the night in Boom Ravine.

The next day was spent in re-organising the battalion, and at 6.00 am 26 August the advance continued. The new objective was the German held positions near the Ligny Tilloy-Luisenhof Farm road.

After passing the first point, the Blue Cut, Greenwood had to lead his battalion over open country with little cover. After four years of fighting much of the countryside had been obliterated. The German machine-gun positions were strongly dug in, and opened fire. The battalion took heavy casualties and after crossing the Yellow Cut was forced to take cover, mostly in shell holes. Patrols were sent out to locate the enemy machine-guns and one company, led by Major Walsh, got within 300 yards of the objective before being forced to withdraw. Owing to high losses over the past few days the remains of 9th KOYLI was organised into one company. A line of posts was established about 300 yards in front of the Yellow Cut and these positions were held during the night of 26/27 August.

Boom Ravine today, the southern end of the ravine looking north with Miraumont on the left side of view. 9th KOYLI advanced left to right across the picture.
(photograph: Dorien Clifford)

Most of the next day was spent taking cover from enemy machine-gun and shell fire. Heavy casualties over the past four days had made any form of advance impossible. At 8.30 that evening the reduced battalion was relieved by the Northumberland Fusiliers, the Pioneer Battalion of 21st Division. 28 August was taken up by re-organising, in divisional reserve, but 9th KOYLI was back in action on 29 August when it was ordered to occupy trenches which had been deserted by the retreating Germans. The enemy was by then in a state of confusion and suffering from low morale.

Meanwhile, the 'friendly fire' wounds that Greenwood had received on 24 August were causing him considerable pain and four days after the event he reluctantly reported sick. He went to the dressing station for treatment for his wounds and handed over command of the battalion to Major Walsh, his second-in-command.

The War Diaries for the 64th Infantry Brigade recorded Greenwood as reporting to hospital on 28 August, but the Battalion War Diaries referred to the date as 29 August. One possible reason for this discrepancy may be that Brigade Diaries were often updated several times during the day while Battalion War Diaries were normally written up by a tired commanding officer, or his deputy, at the end of the day - or the next day.

Most of Greenwood's injuries were internal, with little external sign of the pain he was suffering; this may explain the Brigade War Diary note that he went to hospital "slightly wounded." According to MoD records, however, he also received gunshot and shrapnel wounds to his back and legs. He was on sick leave for almost seven weeks with this "slight" wound.

The advance continued while Greenwood was on sick leave. The Allied Armies persued the Germans towards the Hindenburg Line and the British Fourth Army succeeded in breaking through the defensive positions on 29 September. Once again 9th KOYLI found itself in the front line and continued to suffer severe casualties. Major Walsh, temporarily in command of the battalion, was wounded on 19 September while leading an attack at Villers Guislain. In an action for which he was awarded the DSO, Major Walsh succeeded in driving back an enemy counter-attack and though shot in the leg he urged his men on as he lay on the ground.

For his outstanding leadership and bravery on 23/24 August Lieutenant-Colonel Greenwood was awarded a Bar to his DSO. The award was announced in the third supplement, dated 2 December, to *The London Gazette* of 29 November 1918. The citation read:

For conspicuous gallantry during an attack. Although ill he refused to leave his battalion, and led the first line to the attack, and after being injured by the bursting of a shell captured the first objective. On reaching the second objective he organised his battalion and another, and took up a defensive position from which he beat off two enemy counter-attacks and held his ground until relieved. Next day, when the advance was held up by very heavy machine-gun fire, he made a daring reconnaissance, with the result that he succeeded in getting round the enemy's flank. Throughout he set a splendid example of pluck and devotion to duty to all ranks.

The award and full citation was reported in the *Tottenham and Edmonton Weekly Herald* on Friday 13 December 1918. Harry Greenwood had lived in Tottenham with his parents from 1896 onwards and he was still proudly remembered there years later. Under the heading "The Greenwood family" the report concluded:

Lieutenant-Colonel Greenwood is a member of a fighting Tottenham family of 2 West Road, to whom we referred some time ago. His father and three brothers are serving.

By the time this report on the Bar to the DSO was published Greenwood had taken part in another action which would give the people of Tottenham even more reason to feel proud. Through a series of heroic deeds over a two day period in October that year he had won the Victoria Cross, Britain's highest gallantry award.

Chapter Seven

1918 Ovillers to Grand Gay Farm road

After reluctantly reporting sick with injuries from exploding shells in August Lieutenant-Colonel Greenwood was taken to a casualty clearing station, where his injuries were assessed. From there he was sent to England for treatment and recuperation. He did not return from sick leave until Tuesday 15 October 1918, just eight days before the action that was to earn him the Victoria Cross. He was only a few weeks away from his 37th birthday and was not as young or fit as he used to be, but this did not seem to deter him.

His battalion was then at Walincourt, later moving to Montigny to be ready for the next Allied offensive. The Hindenburg Line had been breached at the end of September and the enemy was in retreat. The German Army had become physically exhausted and its morale was very low. Final victory was less than a month away.

The War Diaries of 9th KOYLI recorded for Monday 21 October 1918:

> *The Commanding Officer today inspected the battalion in fighting order. Afterwards he addressed the men generally and complimented them on the way they had maintained the good traditions of the Regiment. In view of forthcoming operations these remarks were well timed and likely to have a stimulative effect in the next battle.*

In that battle ahead Harry Greenwood was to prove yet again that he was an effective and courageous leader. After the collapse of the Hindenburg Line the German Army retreated to the natural defence lines offered by the many rivers in France and Flanders. These rivers were often dammed to make crossings difficult and all the bridges were destroyed by the retreating Germans. The River Selle, on the Hermann Line, near Le Cateau was finally crossed by the British Third Army on 20 October. A combined Fourth, Third and First Armies operation continued the battle on 23 October, advancing over a wide area between the River Scheldt and the Sambre-Oise canal.

Details of the new offensive were contained in 64th Infantry Brigade Operation Orders no. 213 which were advised to individual battalions on 22 October. The attack was to commence early the next morning. Advancing in a north easterly direction, 21st Division (V Corps, Third Army) was to capture the village of Ovillers and strategic points to the south west of Vendegies-au-Bois. Objectives on the route were designated Red Dotted Line, Red Line, Green Dotted Line, Green Line and Brown Line (see maps 1-3).

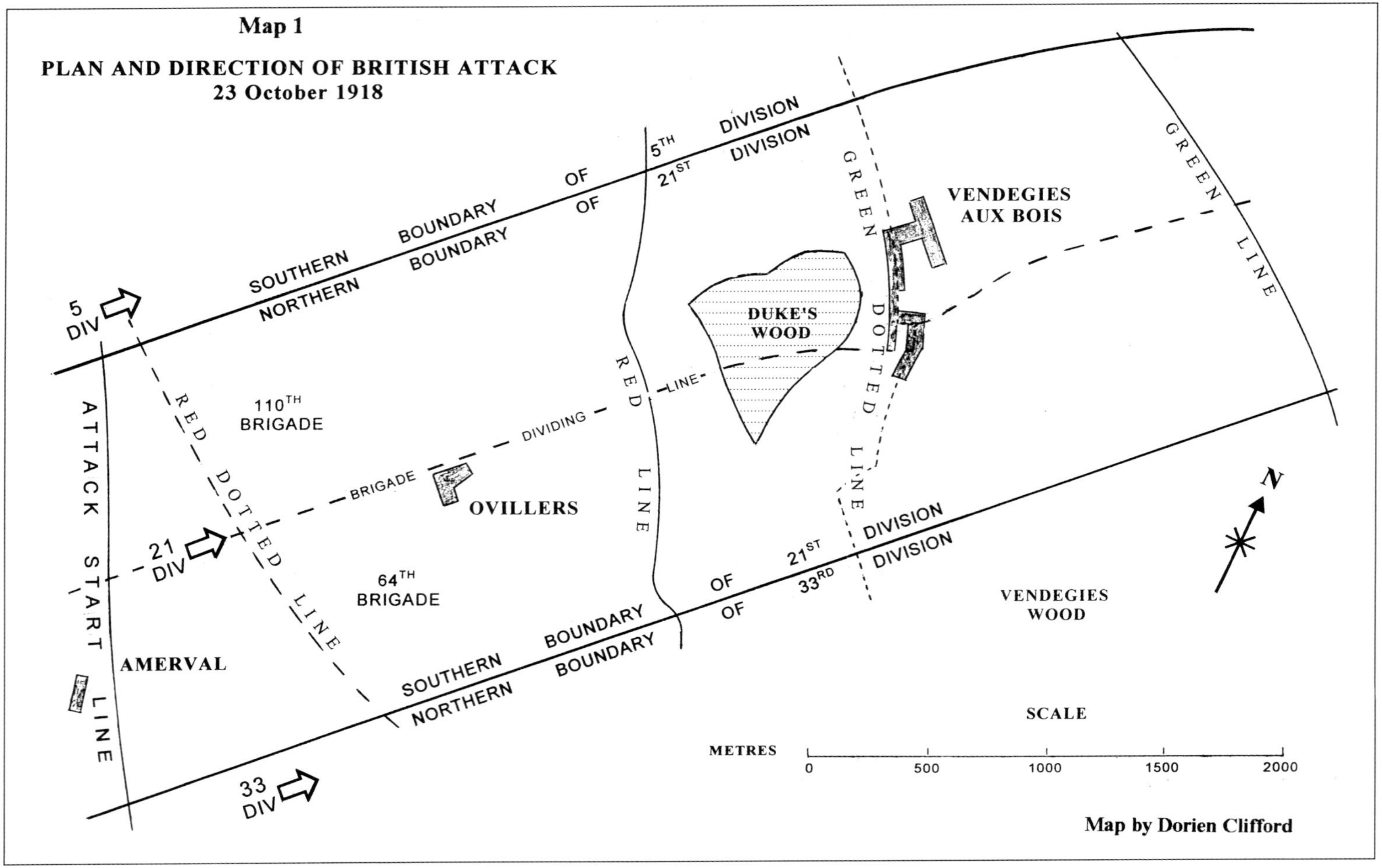

Map 1
PLAN AND DIRECTION OF BRITISH ATTACK
23 October 1918

Map 2

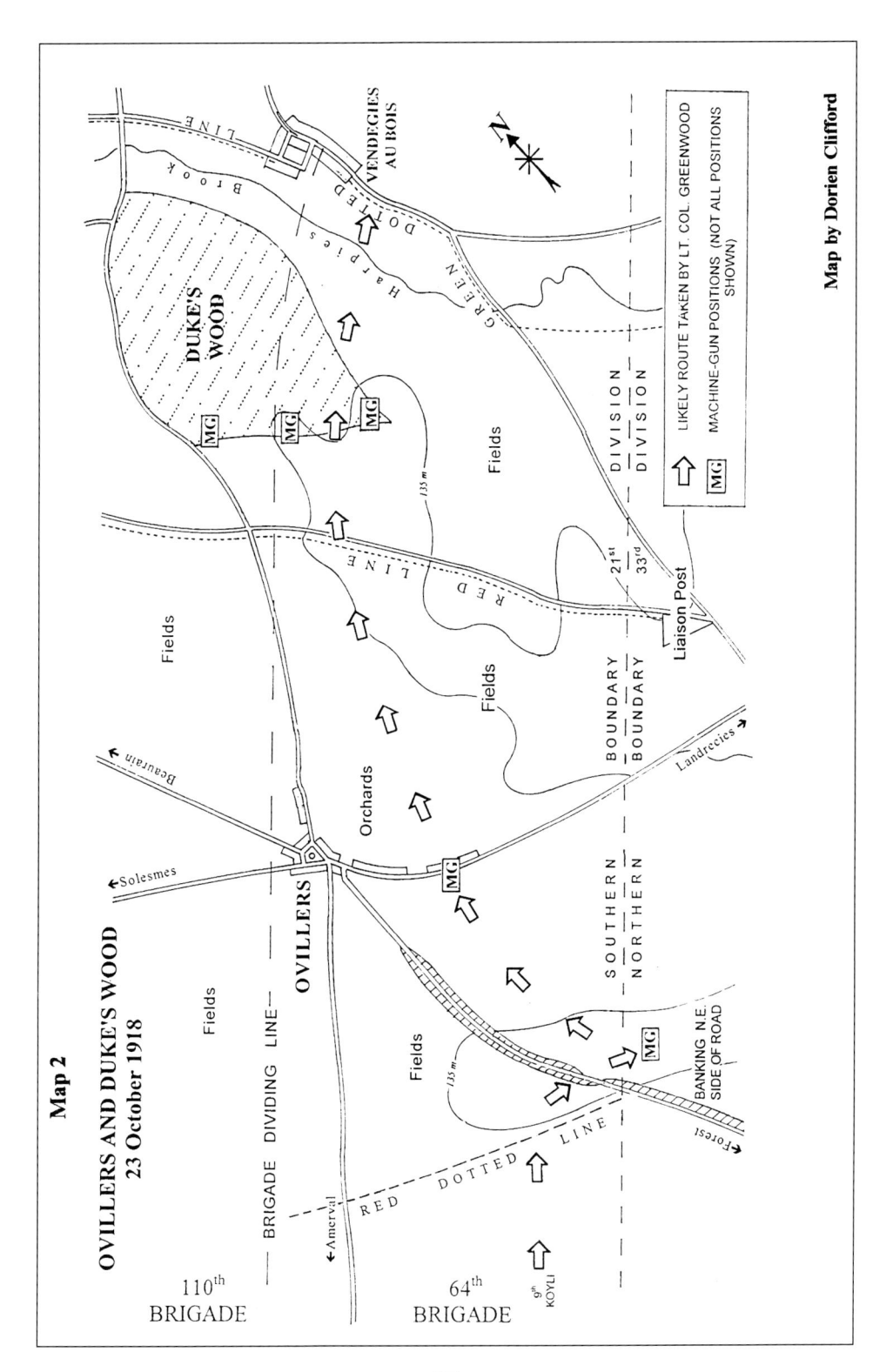

OVILLERS AND DUKE'S WOOD
23 October 1918

Map by Dorien Clifford

Map 3

THE ADVANCE FROM THE GREEN LINE - 24 October 1918

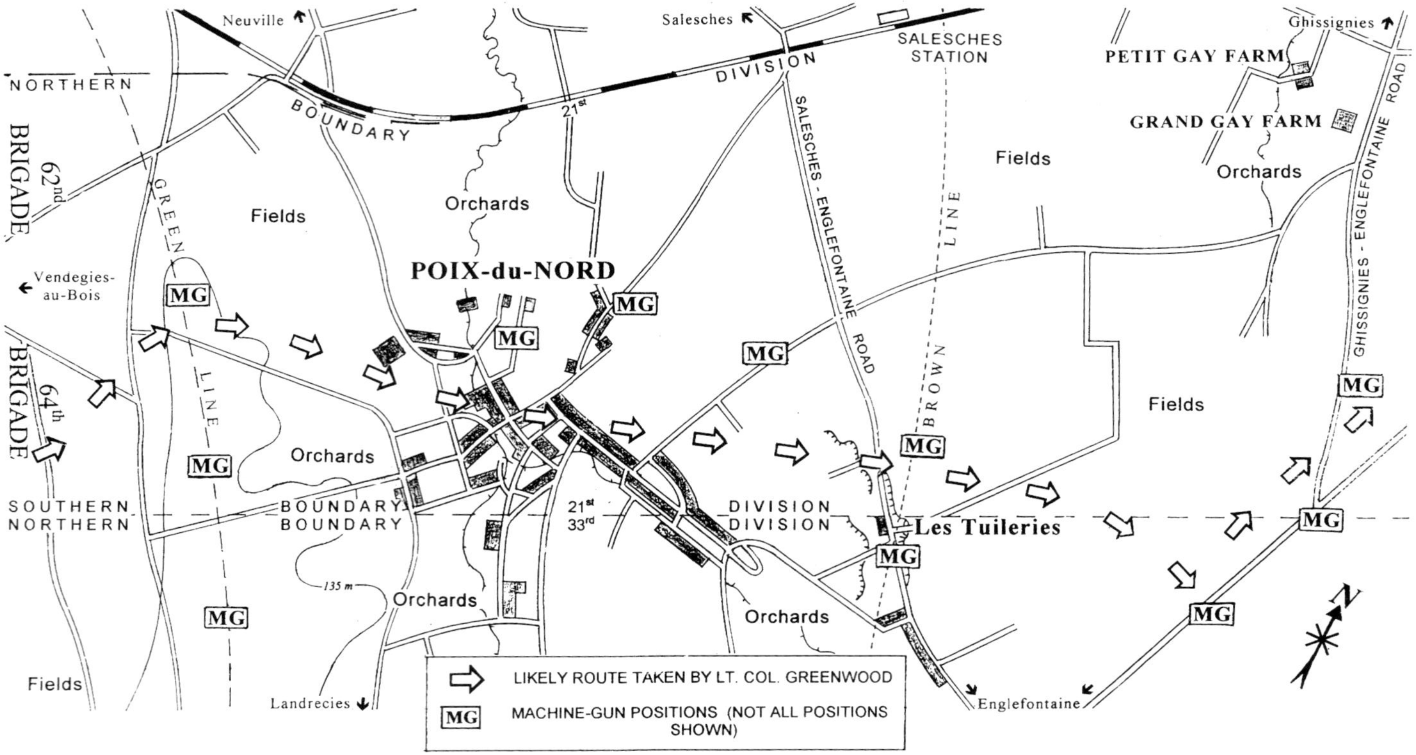

Map by Dorien Clifford

Facing the advancing British Armies were divisions of the German Second Army of Crown Prince Rupprecht's Army Group. The regiments within these divisions cannot positively be identified, however, as most German regimental records were destroyed in the fighting for Berlin in 1945.

There were three brigades in 21st Division during October 1918. 110th Brigade was allocated the left sector and 64th Brigade the right. 62nd Brigade was to follow in support until the Green Dotted Line, when it was to pass through the other two brigades and capture the Green Line and the Brown Line.

Within 64th Brigade 1st East Yorkshires were given the responsibility of capturing north west portions of the Red Dotted Line and Red Line, and mopping up the village of Ovillers. (There is another and better known Ovillers near Albert in the Somme area which is sometimes mistaken for the village near where Greenwood won his VC.) 9th KOYLI, to the right of 1st East Yorkshires, was given the task of capturing the south east portions of the Red Dotted Line, Red Line and Green Dotted Line.

Two companies of 15th DLI were allocated to follow 9th KOYLI and then form up on their left after arriving at the Red Line. Another two companies were to follow close behind 1st East Yorkshires and assist them, if required, in mopping up Ovillers. Further instructions were given regarding roles after the capture of the Green Dotted Line.

9th KOYLI formed the right flank of the division and as such was responsible for establishing liaison posts with the unit on its right, the 19th Infantry Brigade (33rd Division).

During the afternoon of Tuesday 22 October battalions from 64th Brigade, including 9th KOYLI, moved forward, through Inchy, towards the railway embankment to the north east of Neuvilly. (The embankment is still there even though the railway lines have since been removed.) At 11.30 pm they took up their positions along the starting line, the high ground near Amerval (bitter vale). Close to this hamlet is a cemetery where many of the soldiers killed on the first day of the offensive are buried. 9th KOYLI, on the far right of the brigade, started from a point south east of Amerval. This was crossed by a cutting which provided good cover for the waiting troops. The Germans had been expecting a new British offensive and just after midnight started shelling the assembly areas, although not in the sector occupied by Greenwood and his men.

A British barrage of the German positions preceded the offensive and followed the advance throughout the day. This barrage was planned to move at the rate of 100 yards every four minutes. In the Third Army sector the starting time for the attack varied from 2.00 am to 3.20 am depending on the amount of ground to be covered from the start line, which ran in a NNW-SSE direction. Operations were carried out using British time, which then coincided with French time. Zero hour for the 64th Brigade was 2.00 am Wednesday 23 October.

The coloured lines objectives were generally along the crests of ridges, tracks, roads or brooks which would enable them to be easily found, even

Neuvilly embankment today, viewed from the north-west along the line where the railway was in 1918. British troops waited along the embankment before the start of the attack on 23 October 1918.
(photograph: Dorien Clifford)

The small cemetery near Amerval where many British casualties were buried, including a number of KOYLI men killed on the first day of the new offensive.
(photograph: Dorien Clifford)

at night. The first objective, the Red Dotted Line, was achieved without difficulty along the 64th Brigade front by 3.00 am. This was a comparatively easy objective, advancing across slightly undulating countryside mainly open, though neglected, farmland. From the Red Dotted Line the battalions waited and observed the battery on the village and other positions ahead. It was not a defensive line to be captured, more of a re-grouping point, and it was planned to leave the Red Dotted Line approximately 60 minutes after reaching it to allow the barrage to go further ahead. In the Third Army sector there was a ground mist at the commencement of the attack, but this was not thick enough to cover the advancing troops.

Villages and other strategic points were defended by a ring of German machine-gun posts. These were not in the elaborate trench systems seen on the Somme, but mainly simple holes in the ground with sandbag protection for the gunners. Each machine-gun normally had a four man crew, with guns spaced sufficiently far apart to cover a wide field of fire. There would have been machine-gun posts, many of them ringed with barbed wire, on most if not all the routes into Ovillers, with more in the village. All elevated positions in front of Ovillers were ideal positions for concealed machine-guns. Despite being on the run the Germans were usually able to meet their preference for defending heavily fortified high ground. Such was the speed of the Allied advance that the German Army had only a few days to try to fortify the whole area.

Ovillers then, as now, was a small cluster of red brick buildings around a church, with outlying farms and cottages. In 1917 the German Army had demolished the church tower to take the bell for scrap metal. Four years of German occupation had caused considerable damage to

Ovillers church before 1914.
(photograph: Claudine Pardon)

property in Ovillers and Amerval and many of the houses and farm buildings were badly damaged in the shelling which preceded the liberation of these villages. Duez Farm, on the corner of the Amerval road in Ovillers, was further damaged when the retreating Germans exploded a mine in the road. By then the civilian population had been evacuated.

The British advance continued when the barrage lifted at 3.52 am. While they had been waiting for the shelling to stop, units from 64th Brigade took shelter behind the contours of the countryside. When they stood up to move on they were no longer hidden from view. Problems were immediately encountered by 9th KOYLI near Ovillers. Advancing north-eastwards, still across open rolling fields, its progress was halted by an unexpected enemy machine-gun post which had not been mopped up and was causing heavy casualties. Although not yet daylight, there was a bright moon and the advancing British soldiers could be made out moving over the fields in front of Ovillers and easily picked off by the Germans.

The machine-gun post was to their right, most likely on Revenez-Vous-En ridge, with commanding views over the countryside to the south east of the village. It would also have had control over the Ovillers to Forest-en-Cambresis road, a sunken road with embankments both sides. From this elevated position the German gunners would have had a good view of the British troops advancing from the direction of the Red Dotted Line. Sunken roads, a feature of the area, usually made ideal locations for machine-guns but not on that particular stretch of the road. The undulating nature of the countryside in front of it would have restricted the view of any machine-gun crew and deprived them of an efficient field of fire. They needed more height.

Three postcard views of Ovillers 1918, from the collection of Claudine Pardon.

Left: the ruins of Ovillers church. The Germans blew up the bell tower in 1917.

Top and bottom: Buildings at Duez Farm, on the Amerval road in Ovillers, destroyed during the fighting in 1918.

Ovillers today, almost mid-way between the Red Dotted Line and the village. The south-east entrance to Ovillers is on the far right.
(photograph: Dorien Clifford)

Ovillers today, slightly closer than the previous picture, with the dip in front of the village becoming more perceptible.
(photograph: Dorien Clifford)

The Germans had set up their machine-gun in the territory designated to be captured by 5th/6th Scottish Rifles, part of the 19th Infantry Brigade (33rd Division). It is known that the Scottish Rifles had been delayed that morning, particularly around La Croisette and Richemont, and may not have yet reached the position. However, if they had reached there it is possible that they could have missed mopping up the machine-gun post if the Germans were at the time still sheltering from the previous artillery bombardment.

This machine-gun needed to be eliminated quickly in order that the 9th KOYLI advance could continue. Greenwood's VC recommendation stated that the position should have been cleared by "the unit on its right", but there was no time to wait for 19th Brigade to finish the job and so an inter-brigade excursion was planned.

Lieutenant-Colonel Greenwood always believed in leading from the front, and that included attacking enemy machine-guns. Armed with his pistol, and probably a few hand grenades, he went on ahead of his men and attacked the post. It was in darkness, the only available light for the Germans to feed ammunition belts would have been the moon. But Greenwood could see and hear them. The embankments either side of the road in front of Revenez-Vous-En ridge would have provided some cover for Greenwood as he outmanoeuvred the Maxim by waiting until it was completing its firing arc at the furthest point from him. He then rushed forward up the ridge and killed the four man crew. To charge one of these guns, which was "firing at point-blank range", took incredible courage. There was probably also an element of good fortune in that the Germans did not spot him until it was too late. He suddenly appeared out of the darkness and took them by surprise.

The History of the King's Own Yorkshire Light Infantry in the Great War recorded that the machine-gun post "was encountered *west* of Ovillers, half-way between Neuville *(sic)* and Vendegies." If a line were drawn between Neuvilly and Vendegies the half way point would be on top of Haute Montee (Long Way Up) ridge on the Red Dotted Line to the south west of Ovillers. Or the *History* could have meant that Ovillers was a place about half way between Neuvilly and Vendegies. Either way, that machine-gun post would have been too far west to be the one attacked by Greenwood. The Regimental History is the only primary source which places the first machine-gun to the west of the village and it is possible that the writer (or publisher) mistakenly stated west instead of east.

It is well documented that 9th KOYLI advanced on the far right of the brigade (east of Ovillers) and would have been unlikely to cross the enemy held village to attack a machine-gun post to the west.

The 1st East Yorkshires ably dealt with any such threat to their advance. Their War Diaries recorded that the "battalion advanced in direction of Ovillers, C and D companies mopped up the village of Ovillers."

Having eliminated the first machine-gun post Greenwood boldly led his men towards the next objective, the Red Line. His most likely route would have been across country, keeping the Ovillers-Forest road to his left and

The Ovillers-Forest road today. Having eliminated the first machine gun post, Lt. Col. Greenwood made his way across the fields to the right of the road.
(photograph: Dorien Clifford)

heading north before reaching the village to bring him back in line with his battalion's planned position (see map no. 2).

64th Brigade's advance continued but was contested all the way. Considerable artillery and machine-gun fire was encountered around Ovillers and Bois le Duc.

Greenwood's battalion was held up by another machine-gun post near the eastern entrance to Ovillers. The village has contracted in size since 1918 and what was "the entrance to the village" then is surrounded by fields and barns now. It was one of the main entrances to Ovillers - the Ovillers-Forest road at the time being little more than a dirt track. Greenwood took two men from his battalion (described as 'runners', or message carriers, in the VC citation) and set off to eliminate this second machine-gun post. The two men would probably have been chosen for their skill in evading and outmanoeuvreing the enemy when carrying messages. Even so, it could not have been easy for three men to try and outmanoeuvre the post without being seen. It is likely that Greenwood used the two runners as stalkers to distract the enemy's attention while he charged the machine-gun post and killed the crew. For the second time that morning he rushed a German position under the cover of darkness and took the gunners by surprise, killing them all and capturing the gun.

Greenwood's Victoria Cross recommendation made by Brigadier-General C. V. Edwards, CO 64th Infantry Brigade, described the dramatic elimination of the two machine-gun positions:

Ovillers today. The Forest road is on the left by the Fleurs sign and the road from Amerval is at the next junction. This area has been completely rebuilt since 1918. The picture was taken about 200 metres in front of where the second machine-gun post would have been.
(photograph: Dorien Clifford)

Whilst advancing eastwards towards Ovillers (sic) on the early morning of 23rd the advance of the Battalion was checked by an enemy M.G. post which had not been mopped up by the unit on its right and which was causing heavy casualties. Lieut. Col. Greenwood single-handed rushed this M.G. post which was firing at point-blank range, and killed the crew of four. At the entrance of the village of Ovillers, another M.G. post was encountered, which again held up the advance. Again Lt. Col. Greenwood rushed this post with two of his Battalion runners, killing the occupants ...

The War Diaries of 64th Infantry Brigade reported on the fast moving events of the day:

110th Infantry Brigade rang up and reported having seen prisoners coming from Ovillers and our troops north east of the village. Message timed 7.30 am arrived reporting 1st East Yorkshire Regiment and 9th KOYLI 300 yards east of Ovillers and the enemy shelling fairly heavily. Message received from Lt. Col. H. Greenwood DSO. MC. 9th KOYLI timed 7.45 am reporting the Red Line captured and held and troops just starting the final objective - the Green Dotted Line.

Brigade HQ was moved to Ovillers later in the day, with 9th KOYLI HQ moving to Vendegies-au-Bois shortly after its capture that morning. Three tanks were detailed to assist the division in the clearing of Ovillers as soon as there was sufficient light. Following the infantry, they worked round the outer edge of the village to help wipe out the remaining machine-gun positions. One of the tanks afterwards fell into a gravel pit, the second broke a track and the third lost direction in the dark and strayed into another divisional area. It had been planned for the tanks to move forward and, provided that they could cross the River Harpies, assist 62nd Brigade in the capture of the Green and Brown Lines.

The British barrage was timed to reach the Red Line, the Beaurain-Slaughter House road, at 5.04 am. 9th KOYLI captured its section of this objective shortly after. The exact time is not recorded, but it is known that 15th DLI, following behind 9th KOYLI, reached the Line at 5.16 am. News of the capture of this second objective was not received at Brigade HQ until 7.45 am, indicating that Greenwood had sent one of his 'runners' back on foot. When the barrage lifted at 7.08 am the advance continued. It was daylight by then, dawn having started to appear at 6.20 am.

Beyond the Red Line was Bois le Duc (Duke's Wood), a diamond shaped wooded area around the local chateau. Greenwood led the forward line of his battalion to the western tip of the wood, which was known to be heavily defended. This wooded area made ideal cover for machine-guns and also artillery and, unfortunately for the attacking force, the barrage had failed to destroy all these enemy positions. By the time they reached Duke's Wood 9th KOYLI had lost contact with both flank units. 19th Brigade, to the right, had been held up and did not reach its part of the Red Line until 7.30 am. Because of casualties and leaving one company behind to man flank and liaison posts, Greenwood's battalion numbered only 250 men and at this stage of the battle they appear to have over-stretched themselves.

This small unit suddenly found itself "almost surrounded by hostile machine-gun posts" and the Germans counter-attacked and broke through on the right flank, where they are believed to have had troops positioned on high ground. The enemy managed to get within 40 yards of 9th KOYLI before their courageous Commanding Officer rallied his men and the attack was repulsed.

Heeding the Regimental motto "Cede Nullis" (Yield to None) the battalion successfully fought its way out and pushed back the enemy attack. Led by Lieutenant-Colonel Greenwood his men charged forward, cheering as they ran through Duke's Wood. 9th KOYLI chased after the retreating Germans and captured the third and final battalion objective of the day - the Green Dotted Line, which roughly followed the course of the River Harpies, (now no more than a brook) in front of Vendegies-au-Bois.

In doing so the battalion captured 150 Germans and a large amount of enemy equipment, including eight machine-guns and one field gun - a remarkable feat for such a small isolated unit.

The remaining machine-guns in Duke's Wood continued to cause severe casualties among the attacking force. 6th Leicestershire Regiment (110th Brigade) met considerable opposition in the attack on the Green Dotted Line, mainly from Duke's Wood.

East of Ovillers, at the liaison post (edge of field by hawthorn tree) marking the boundary with 33rd Division to the right of 21st Division.
(photograph: Dorien Clifford)

Greenwood's battalion stopped at the Green Dotted Line, which was captured by 8.05 am, and 62nd Infantry Brigade passed through to continue the advance. 15th DLI took over this line, with 9th KOYLI and 1st East Yorkshires forming a defensive flank. Vendegies-au-Bois was captured by 62nd Brigade late morning and was said to have completely 'mopped up' the town by 12.55 pm. After the capture of Vendegies-au-Bois 64th Brigade moved forward in support. In the afternoon of 23 October the Germans retreated to the Green Line and there was considerable artillery fire from this position, causing heavy casualties. 62nd Brigade later reached and attacked this defended line, capturing part of it.

21st Division recorded that at 3.45 pm 23 October:

62nd Infantry Brigade reported that the fourth objective, the Green Line, had been captured. Two companies on the right were advancing towards Poix du Nord. Troops of 33rd Division could be seen on high ground to the right.

The many orchards and hedges between Vendegies and Poix du Nord made it difficult to locate the German artillery, which continued to shell the British lines. Much of the ground was similar to the 'bocage' country of Normandy that slowed down the Allied advance in 1944. By the end of the day the advance had been stalled and British troops were consolidating their positions along the road just south of the Green Line.

The Times followed the day's action and reported in its edition of 24 October 1918:

The attack this morning was delivered by English and Scottish troops of the Third and Fourth Armies between the Sambre Canal and the River Scheldt, south of Valenciennes.

The advance was made over country rendered difficult by many streams, villages, and woods, which were defended by the enemy with much resolution. During the period of assembly and early stages of the battle, hostile artillery displayed great activity with high explosive and gas shells.

Throughout the day's operations, our troops have fought their way forward in spite of obstinate resistance, especially by the enemy's artillery and machine-guns.

On the evening of 23 October 64th Brigade received orders for an attack on Poix du Nord, to take place the following morning. The brigade was to capture the main part of the town. The suburbs to the south were in the area allocated to 33rd Division, and were to be captured by units from that division. Over to the left, 37th Division had replaced 5th Division at the Green Dotted Line. After Poix du Nord 64th Brigade had two main objectives: the Salesches-Englefontaine road and the Ghissignies-Englefontaine road (see map no. 3).

At 4.00 am on 24 October 62nd and 64th Infantry Brigades launched a combined attack on the Green Line, under a covering barrage. 110th Brigade was in support. The advance continued with 15th DLI on the left flank of 64th Brigade and 9th KOYLI on the right.

During an attack on the Green Line, south of Poix du Nord, 64th Brigade was held up by enemy machine-gun fire from positions on high ground beyond the road. In the 9th KOYLI sector the battalion was delayed for two hours in front of some wired defences. Frustrated at being kept back, Greenwood decided to carry out a personal reconnaissance and cautiously edged his way towards the enemy-held positions. He discovered a weak spot in the defences. Part of the ridge was held by a solitary machine-gun, which was not linked to the other gun positions. Single handed he crept forward and then rushed the post from a distance of approximately 20 yards. As daylight was breaking, Greenwood charged the machine-gun, captured the isolated position and killed the gun crew.

Whether Greenwood should have continued to put his life at risk in close combat of this nature is debatable. As the most senior officer in 9th KOYLI his loss would have been felt far greater than if an NCO or private had been sent in. But he was aware of the risks involved to himself and his battalion, and as Commanding Officer the decision to attack the machine-gun posts was his.

Having eliminated the machine-gun and crew, he was then able to lead his battalion, and allow the brigade to follow, through the gap he had

Duke's Wood today, to the west of the Wood looking due east about 50 metres short of the Red Line. (photograph: Dorien Clifford)

created. He then charged across the Green Line and on towards Poix du Nord. The other machine-guns were sufficiently far away for the battalion to avoid casualties, and these guns were captured by other units. The Green Line along the whole divisional front was captured soon afterwards (see map no. 3).

Considerable opposition was met in Poix du Nord and a large number of the enemy were killed. The town was taken by 8.00 am and 64th Brigade HQ moved in at 2.30 pm. Poix du Nord was full of French civilians so no British shelling of this objective had been permitted. Over 2,500 civilians were found to be still living there, but this did not prevent the Germans from shelling the town once it was in British hands.

From Poix du Nord the advance continued to the Salesches-Englefontaine road, a sunken road, where the Germans put up a fierce resistance. 9th KOYLI suffered heavy losses but Greenwood inspired his battalion to repel an enemy counter-attack and push through the German defences.

Brigadier-General C. V. Edwards in his Victoria Cross recommendation continued:

The whole flank of M.G. posts was turned and the advance proceeded through Poix du Nord, the Battalion led by Col. Greenwood sweeping aside a further line of M.G. posts that was encountered north of the town, reaching its objective with both its flanks in the air. Heavy M.G. and field gun fire was then opened against the Battalion from the front and right flank. Heavy casualties were caused, the line wavered, and it was only by Col. Greenwood walking up and down in front of the advanced posts (under heavy M.G. fire in full view of the enemy) encouraging his men that the line was held and an enemy counter-attack beaten off...

Just beyond the Salesches-Englefontaine road was the Brown Line, which followed the crest of a hill on the high ground behind the road. The Brown Line was reached, and captured, despite the many enemy machine-gun positions in the area. Around Les Tuileries (named after the many tileworks in the area), near 21st Division's southern boundary, there were numerous earthworks and clay pits which created further obstacles for the attacking forces.

Only one more objective remained for that day - the capture of the road running south east from Grand Gay Farm (the Ghissignies-Englefontaine road). Both 62nd and 64th Brigades had tried without success to reach this objective and encountered very heavy machine-gun and artillery fire. A further attack, with supporting barrage, was arranged for 4.00 pm. British field artillery commenced shelling a line 300 yards in front of the Les Tuileries-Salesches road and lifted twelve minutes later to enable the infantry to advance. As the troops moved forward so did the barrage, which advanced at a rate of 100 yards every three minutes until 300 yards beyond the objective and then ceased. The barrage then moved to the orchards to the west, where the Germans had their artillery, and to the high ground beyond the Ghissignies-Englefontaine road. Between the Brown Line and the final objective were fields, containing enemy machine-gun positions.

62nd Brigade was on the left and 64th Brigade on the right of the attack. Within the latter brigade, 15th DLI advanced on the left and 1st East Yorkshires on the right. 9th KOYLI, which had been at the front of the fighting over the previous two days, was in support. The battalion was given the important task of guarding the right flank of the brigade and the division.

Good progress was made and the objective was reached by 6.00 pm. But not without difficulty - Greenwood again found his right flank unprotected when the brigade from the next divisional sector was not in place. 64th Brigade noted, without further comment, in its War Diaries that "the situation on our right remained somewhat obscure."

Enemy machine-gun posts were firing on the exposed flank of the 64th Brigade, with 9th KOYLI being in the firing line. Greenwood led his battalion forward and eliminated all the hostile machine-gun posts. To prevent further incidents he then captured an objective well to the right of the allotted boundary for his battalion or 64th Brigade - not for the first time since battle had re-commenced on 23 October.

It would have been with a certain sense of satisfaction that he handed the captured objective over to the division on his right when it had caught up with his advance (perhaps not surprisingly there is no mention of this in the War Diaries of 33rd Division). By taking this additional position Greenwood had not only secured the right flank of his own battalion, but

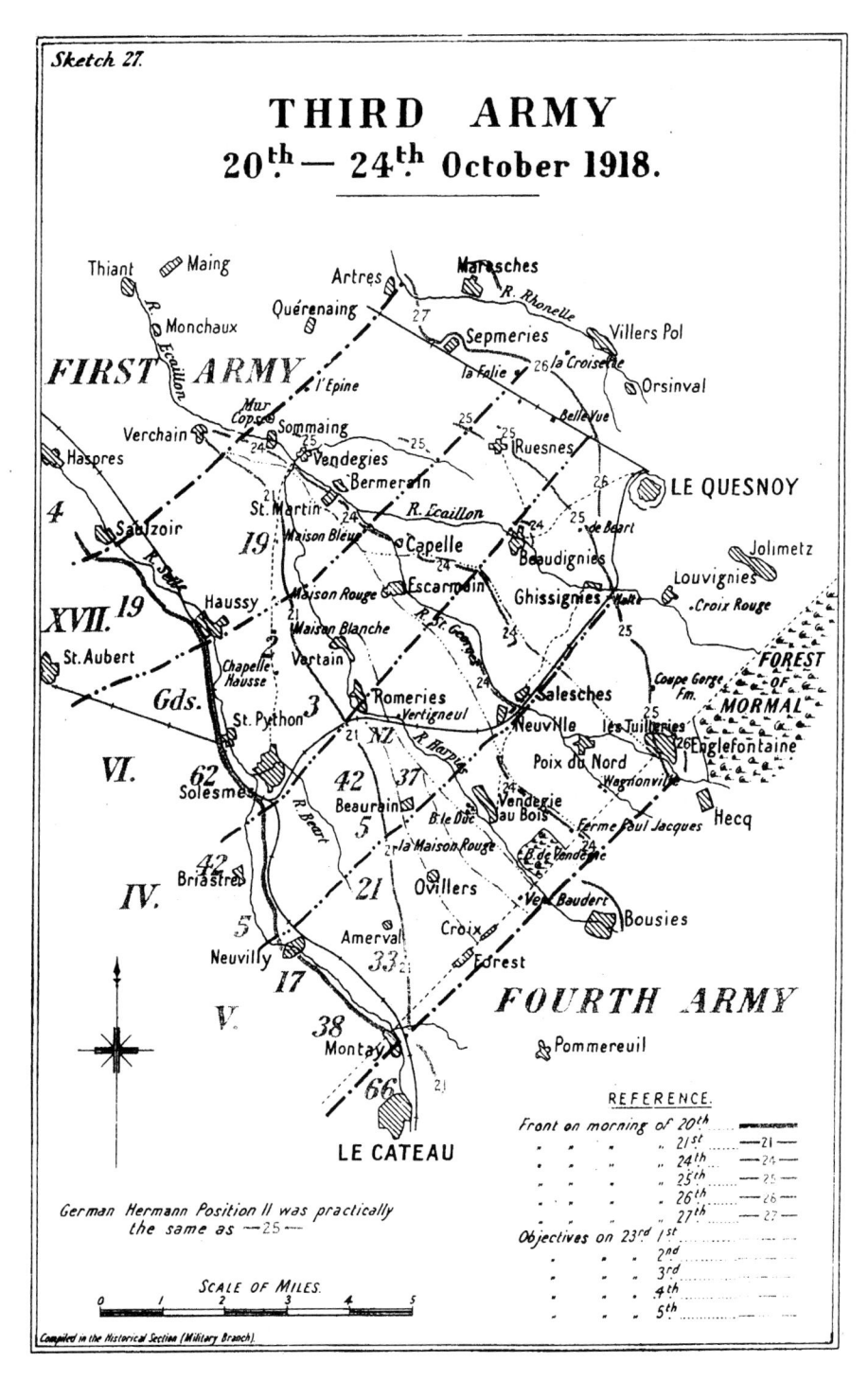

Reproduced from *History of the Great War. Military Operations France & Belgium, 1914-1918.*
Compiled by Brigadier-General Sir James Edmonds.
HMSO 1922-1949.

also the 64th Brigade and the whole 21st Division. Since 2.00 am the previous day the division had advanced approximately three and a half miles.

The final objective of 24 October, the Ghissignies-Englefontaine road, and also Grand Gay Farm had been held in considerable strength but the Germans retreated on the approach of the British infantry. That evening 62nd and 64th Brigades dug in and made a defensive position in case of a German counter-attack, but there was little enemy activity.

Brigadier-General Edwards summed up Greenwood's courageous conduct in his VC recommendation:

During the two days fighting Col. Greenwood, by the magnificent example he set his officers and men showing utter contempt for danger, contributed greatly towards the success of the operations during the advance... His conduct and example during the fighting was beyond all praise.
(The VC recommendation has not been quoted in full to avoid repetition.)

9th KOYLI casualties had been high over the two day period 23/24 October. Greenwood himself did not escape injury, which is hardly surprising in view of his high profile leadership. He was hit several times by shrapnel from shells falling near him and was twice blown off his feet. On one occasion he was badly stunned by an exploding shell. None of this had any effect on his determination to lead his battalion to victory. This was not the first time that Greenwood had been wounded. He had been seriously injured in action in August and had only been back from sick leave for just over a week.

64th Brigade was relieved by 51st Brigade on 25 October and withdrew from the front line to billets in Vendegies-au-Bois, later moving back to Inchy. Here the battalions rested and re-organised, making up their numbers from new drafts of men just arrived from the UK. The action around Poix du Nord on 24 October was to be 9th Battalion's last full scale attack of the war.

Lieutenant-Colonel Greenwood inspected the new ranks of 9th KOYLI on 28 October and told them of the proud traditions of the battalion. Newcomers would have been forgiven for thinking that their Commanding Officer rushing enemy machine-gun posts was one of those traditions. The following day 9th KOYLI moved back to billets in Vendegies for six days of training.

Harry Greenwood's heroic actions and fine leadership qualities were recognised by senior officers in his brigade. On 29 October Brigadier-General Edwards recommended him for the Victoria Cross, and two days later sent the completed Army Form W 3121 up the line for approval.

As the Allied Armies continued to push back the Germans there was a general feeling that the end of the war was near. This did not affect the

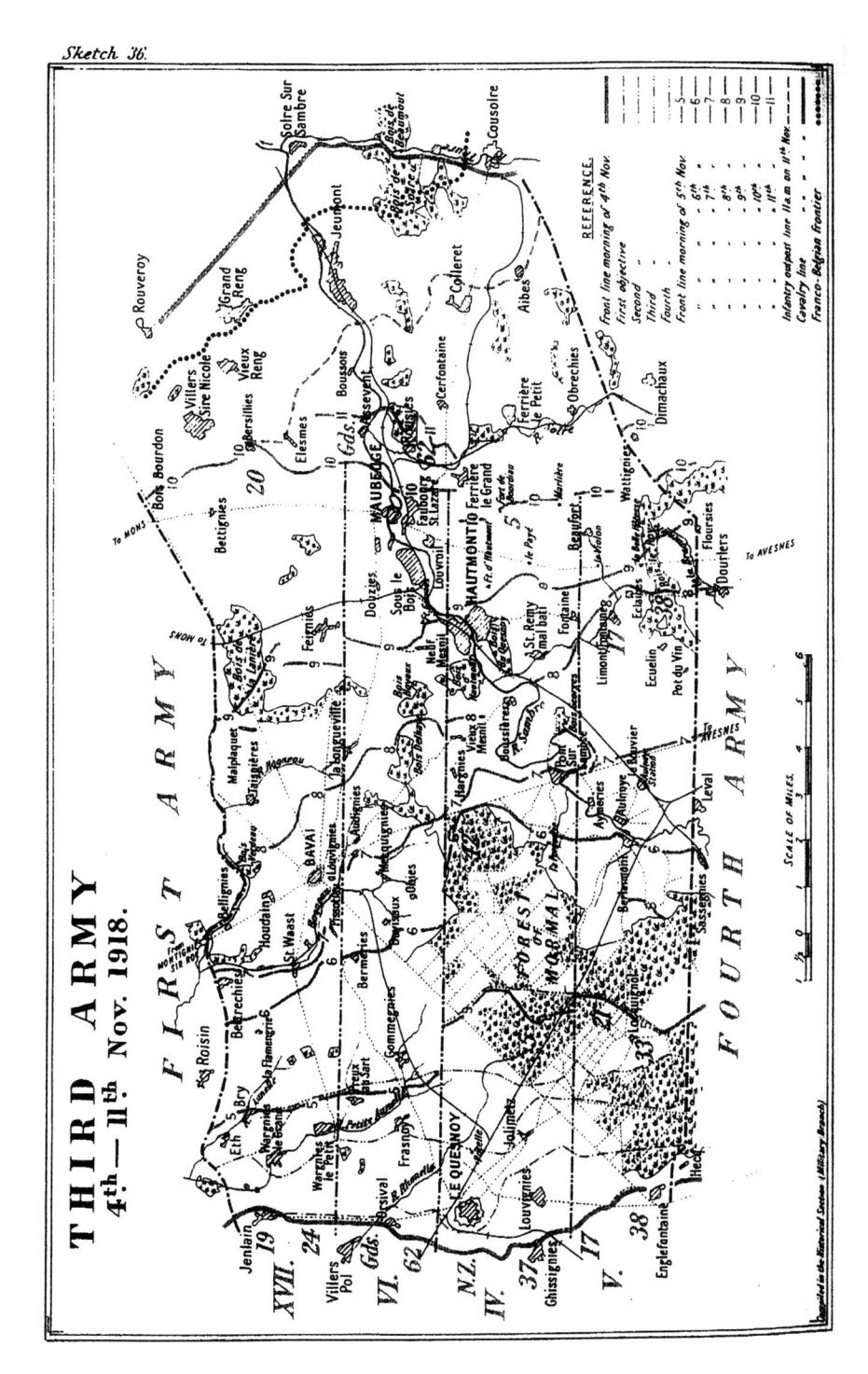

Reproduced from *History of the Great War. Military Operations France & Belgium, 1914-1918.*
Compiled by Brigadier-General Sir James Edmonds.
HMSO 1922-1949.

efficiency of the British Army, which remained as resolute as ever. 64th Brigade, as part of a combined Fourth, Third and First Armies operation, advanced eastward again on 4 November, with 9th KOYLI being a support battalion. The Forest of Mormal was taken on 5 November and that evening 64th Brigade had reached the west bank of the River Sambre. Crossings were made overnight and the advance continued towards Limont-Fontaine, with 9th KOYLI once more in the front line.

Previous Allied offensives, such as the Somme in 1916 and Passchendaele in 1917, were restricted to specific areas. The offensive in October/November 1918 involved all the Allied Armies across the whole Western Front. With the Belgians to the north of British and Empire troops and the French and Americans to the south, substantial territorial gains were made in the final weeks of the war.

Germany had lost the initiative and it was obvious to the German High Command that the war could not be won. After four years of war the fighting spirit of the country had been worn down by attrition and the morale of the army was falling daily. Crown Prince Rupprecht was quoted in *History of the Great War, Military Operations France and Belgium 1918* as reporting that "our troops are exhausted and their numbers have dwindled terribly. The number of infantry in an active division is seldom as much as 3,000."

In early October 1918 the German Government made appeals for an immediate armistice to the American President, Woodrow Wilson. An exchange of messages followed but Wilson made it clear that the Allies would not enter into armistice talks with the present military leaders. To allow negotiations to continue, General Ludendorff resigned as Army Chief-of-Staff on 27 October. In a further sign that the war was lost the German High Seas Fleet mutinied two days later.

The final collapse followed swiftly. Germany's allies concluded separate ceasefires - Turkey on 30 October and Austria on 3 November. A socialist government came to power in Germany and declared the country a republic. As a result the Kaiser was forced to abdicate on 9 November and went into exile in Holland to avoid arrest. Field Marshal Hindenburg remained as overall army commander, and after several days of negotiations a German armistice was arranged for Monday 11 November 1918, to be effective from 11.00 am French time.

9th KOYLI were marching towards Limont-Fontaine when the news of the armistice was received. The Battalion War Diaries for 11 November recorded that:

En route news of the signing of the Armistice arrived, and while inward satisfaction was undoubtedly felt, no outward demonstration was made.

With the war over, further good news soon followed for the battalion - its Commanding Officer, Lieutenant-Colonel Greenwood, was to be awarded the Victoria Cross.

Chapter Eight

Victoria Cross

News of Greenwood's Victoria Cross award was advised to his battalion just over a week before it was officially promulgated in *The London Gazette*.

The Regimental History of KOYLI recorded:

December 18 1918 proved to be a day of supreme gratification in the history of the 9th KOYLI. The Battalion was notified that the VC, the blue riband of the fighting forces, was conferred on Lt. Col. Harry Greenwood in recognition of his services on October 23 and 24. Every officer and man of the battalion was intensely proud to learn that their leader had been so signally rewarded, and all had a right to feel that beyond the personal recognition the honour was intended to apply to all ranks of this famous fighting battalion.

In the absence of Brigadier-General C. V. Edwards DSO, who was on 22 days leave in England, Lieutenant-Colonel Greenwood had assumed command of the 64th Infantry Brigade on 14 December. He was still at Brigade HQ, then at Pissy, when news of the Victoria Cross award came through, and a telegram was sent to him conveying the hearty congratulations of all the officers and other ranks of the battalion. Although temporarily in command of the brigade he did not receive promotion to Brigadier-General, either acting or temporary.

Lieutenant-Colonel Greenwood VC had the respect and confidence of the entire battalion, and his men would have followed him anywhere he led them. Major Walsh, the second-in-command of the battalion who was back from sick leave, paid his own tribute in the Battalion War Diaries on the day the award was announced:

If the distinction was great so was the rejoicing. Honour had been bestowed on the Commanding Officer, thus honour had come to the Battalion and the Battalion felt a thrill of reflected glory. In battle Col. Greenwood is ever in front with his men. For him to be in rear in action is to be out of it. That useful work may be done from the rear he does not deny, but coupled with this belief he holds other views. For him there is only one position, that is in the van. He does not urge, he leads.

A total of nine Victoria Crosses were awarded to men serving in the King's Own Yorkshire Light Infantry - eight of these during the First World War.

Numb. 31082.

15117

SUPPLEMENT TO
The London Gazette.

Of TUESDAY, the 24th of DECEMBER, 1918.

Published by Authority.

The Gazette is registered at the General Post Office for transmission by Inland Post as a newspaper. The postage rate to places within the United Kingdom, for each copy, is one halfpenny for the first 6 ozs., and an additional halfpenny for each subsequent 6 ozs. or part thereof. For places abroad the rate is a halfpenny for every 2 ounces, except in the case of Canada, to which the Canadian Magazine Postage rate applies.

THURSDAY, 26 DECEMBER, 1918.

War Office,
26th December, 1918.

His Majesty the KING has been graciously pleased to approve of the award of the Victoria Cross to the undermentioned Officers, N.C.O.'s and Men:—

T./Maj. (A./Lt.-Col.) Harry Greenwood, D.S.O., M.C., 9th Bn., K.O. Yorks. L.I.·

For most conspicuous bravery, devotion to duty and fine leadership on the 23rd/24th October, 1918. When the advance of his battalion on the 23rd October was checked, and many casualties caused by an enemy machine-gun post, Lt.-Col. Greenwood single-handed rushed the post and killed the crew. At the entrance to the village of Ovillers, accompanied by two battalion runners, he again rushed a machine-gun post and killed the occupants.

On reaching the objective west of Duke's Wood his command was almost surrounded by hostile machine-gun posts, and the enemy at once attacked his isolated force. The attack was repulsed, and, led by Lt.-Col. Greenwood, his troops swept forward and captured the last objective, with 150 prisoners, eight machine guns and one field gun.

During the attack on the Green Line, south of Poix Du Nord, on 24th October, he again displayed the greatest gallantry in rushing a machine-gun post, and he showed conspicuously good leadership in the handling of his command in the face of heavy fire. He inspired his men in the highest degree, with the result that the objective was captured, and, in spite of heavy casualties, the line was held.

During the further advance on Grand Gay Farm Road, on the afternoon of 24th October, the skilful and bold handling of his battalion was productive of most important results, not only in securing the flank of his brigade, but also in safeguarding the flank of the Division.

His valour and leading during two days of fighting were beyond all praise.

Maj. Blair Anderson Wark, D.S.O., 32nd Bn., A.I.F.

For most conspicuous bravery, initiative and control during the period 29th Sept. to 1st Oct. 1918, in the operations against the Hindenburg Line at Bellicourt and the ad-

Only one VC was to the 9th Battalion (see Appendix II). Lieutenant-Colonel Greenwood was the most decorated KOYLI soldier of the war.

His Victoria Cross was officially announced on Boxing Day, in a supplement dated 26 December to *The London Gazette* of 24 December 1918. The citation read:

His Majesty The King has been graciously pleased to approve of the award of the Victoria Cross to the undermentioned Officers, NCOs and Men:

Temporary Major (Acting Lieutenant Colonel) Harry Greenwood, DSO, MC, 9th Bn. K.O. Yorks L.I. For most conspicuous bravery, devotion to duty and fine leadership on 23/24 October, 1918. When the advance of his battalion on 23 October was checked, and many casualties caused by an enemy machine-gun post, Lt. Col. Greenwood single-handed rushed the post and killed the crew. At the entrance to the village of Ovillers, accompanied by two battalion runners, he again rushed a machine-gun post and killed the occupants.

On reaching the objective west of Duke's Wood his command was almost surrounded by hostile machine-gun posts, and the enemy at once attacked his isolated force. The attack was repulsed, and, led by Lt. Col. Greenwood, his troops swept forward and captured the last objective, with 150 prisoners, eight machine-guns and one field gun. During the attack on the Green Line, south of Poix du Nord, on 24 October, he again displayed the greatest gallantry in rushing a machine-gun post, and he showed conspicuously good leadership in the handling of his command in the face of heavy fire. He inspired his men in the highest degree, with the result that the objective was captured, and, in spite of heavy casualties, the line was held.

During the further advance on Grand Gay Farm Road, on the afternoon of 24 October, the skilful and bold handling of his battalion was productive of most important results, not only in securing the flank of his brigade, but also in safe-guarding the flank of the Division.

His valour and leading during two days of fighting were beyond all praise.

There can be no doubting Harry Greenwood's courage, and he certainly earned his VC the hard way. Decorations or medals for actions over a period of days are not uncommon, of course, nor is two days an exceptional period of time. All Victoria Cross winners are considered to be equal, but any *one* of these heroic deeds might have won another man the coveted award. By date of action, his VC was the 1,133rd to be awarded since 1856.

Greenwood was aware of the great honour being bestowed upon him. As the son of a soldier he also knew the history of the Victoria Cross, how

On the same day that Greenwood's VC was announced, the Daily Sketch *published the above photograph with the caption:* "*Acting Lieut. Col. H Greenwood, whose gallant exploits which won him the VC are told on a news page. He had already won the DSO and the MC.*"
(*photograph:* Daily Sketch*)*

Queen Victoria had taken a personal interest in the design of the new decoration and that the Crosses were made of bronze from cannons captured at Sebastopol during the Crimean War.

The Times reported on all the recently announced VC awards in its edition of 27 December, under the heading "Twelve new VCs. Heroic deeds in the Great Advance." Under a sub-heading "Attacks on machine-gun posts" it detailed the VC citation for Lieutenant-Colonel Greenwood and then, in descending order of seniority, the citations for the other eleven VC recipients. Many other newspapers reported on the new VC awards. The *Daily Sketch* told of the "Colonel's great deeds" and also published a picture of a jovial Harry Greenwood outside Buckingham Palace.

The following day Greenwood was again mentioned in *The London Gazette*, in a supplement to the edition of 27 December, dated 28 December 1918. He was included in "Sir Douglas Haig's Despatch... submitting names deserving of special mention." The number of times Harry Greenwood was mentioned in despatches (MID) is not known for certain, but it is at least twice. Army Lists for 1919 and also 1920 show two mentions - January 1916 and December 1918. MoD records suggest that there may be three. The third MID is thought to have been in January 1917, but there is a question mark against this date.

It is most likely that the then Major Greenwood was mentioned in Field Marshal Viscount French's Despatch of 31 December 1916, but his name was not included with those published in *The London Gazette* of 23 January 1917. A search of the indexes of *The London Gazette* has not revealed the third MID.

Harry Greenwood claimed in his *Who's Who* entry to have been mentioned in despatches three times. It is almost certain, therefore, that he did receive three MIDs, although the dates of only two of these can be verified.

There also appears to be some disagreement about the number of times he was wounded during the war. When he met the King in May 1919 to receive his VC Greenwood wore two stripes on the lower left sleeve of his tunic, to show the number of times he had been wounded while on active service. However, another photograph taken some time after the end of the war shows Greenwood with four wound stripes on his KOYLI uniform. Two of these occasions would have been 24 August 1918 (Bar to DSO action) and 23/24 October 1918 (VC action). The others are not recorded and Greenwood's medical files with the MoD are incomplete. Many sources, most notably Greenwood's own *Who's Who* entry, report that he was "wounded thrice."

The *Tottenham and Edmonton Weekly Herald* in its weekly edition dated Friday 3 January 1919 reported the VC award and full citation. Two weeks later it gave more details of Lieutenant-Colonel Greenwood's background:

Thirty seven years of age, Lieut-Col Greenwood is the eldest son of Yeoman of the Guard Charles Greenwood, who lives at 2 West Road, Tottenham but who is, for the time being, at Llandudno... The Greenwood family have been residents of Tottenham since 1896... Lieut-Col Greenwood lived with his parents till his marriage seven years ago (sic).

Local communities were extremely proud of their own Victoria Cross winners and wanted to be associated with them. In Greenwood's case the expression "a member of a Tottenham fighting family" was used frequently in the local press. A later report mentioned "Two Tottenham men who are members of this most enviable order," the other man being Private Robert Cruickshank from Harringay. The Victoria Cross is, of course, a decoration not an order.

Like many other VC winners before him (and indeed since) Harry Greenwood was genuinely surprised to receive the Victoria Cross. It had not been expected or planned - he was just doing his duty.

Thirty years later another 9th KOYLI officer (L.D.S.) recalled Greenwood's reaction to the news of the VC award in an obituary tribute:

He believed in banging the big drum on behalf of those he commanded - there were no men in the world like his men, though he was not unaware that if glory shone on those he commanded, the spotlight must fall on the leader. But he had a generosity of mind and spirit which produced at times a modesty that was humbling. When shown the letter announcing his Victoria Cross, he was silent for some moments unable to realise the great distinction he had achieved. We waited for his reaction. "This should have been given to W," he said quietly, naming a fellow officer, who earned a DSO during the same period of action, and the tribute was sincere and simple.

L.D.S. was Captain Lancelot Dykes Spicer DSO, MC and Bar, Brigade Major 64th Infantry Brigade. Educated at Rugby and Trinity College, Cambridge he received his first commission in the army in September 1914. He served with 9th KOYLI and was promoted to Temporary Captain in July 1916, before being transferred to Brigade HQ in April 1918.

The officer mentioned (W) was almost certainly Major Theobald Alfred Walsh DSO and Bar, who had assumed command of the battalion when Greenwood was on sick leave. He was a career officer and had served with the Somerset Light Infantry before being attached to 9th KOYLI as second-in-command. Major Walsh was a soldier very much in the Greenwood mould. He led from the front, inspiring his men to reach their objectives, and he had been wounded on both occasions he was awarded the DSO.

Such modesty on Harry Greenwood's part is typical of those heroes chosen to receive the nation's highest award "for valour." There is always someone else who should have been rewarded, and for every hero honoured there must be many more who are overlooked. As Winston Churchill later said about the difficult task of drawing up regulations for such awards: "It is not possible to satisfy everybody without running the risk of satisfying nobody."

With the war over 9th KOYLI, billeted at Fontaine and later at Seux, looked forward to going home. November and December 1918, and the early part of 1919, were spent in recreational and educational duties, with parades and football matches organised to fill the time. The battalion's determination to succeed was extended to the sports field, and in November teams from 9th KOYLI came first in the brigade football and cross country running competitions. On Christmas Eve a brigade ceremonial parade was held, with Lieutenant-Colonel Greenwood in command. The parade proved successful despite the fact that the battalion had not carried out any parade work for some time.

The Battalion War Diaries for Christmas Day 1918 recorded:

Considerable preparation had been made to enable all ranks in the battalion to spend a happy peaceful Xmas. Owing to the forethought of the commanding officer and others, generous supplies of Xmas Fare had been obtained.

Thursday 26 December 1918 was "proclaimed a general holiday in the battalion" in honour of the Victoria Cross award to Lieutenant-Colonel Greenwood, which was officially announced that day in *The London Gazette*.

The huge task of demobilisation took time to organise and the battalion was asked, by Brigade HQ, to show patience while waiting for final release. When the time came to part, Harry Greenwood was sorry to leave the men with whom he had forged such a strong personal link. But he was thankful to have survived a war which had claimed the lives of millions of others, and that he would soon be reunited with his family.

Demobilisation of the armed forces continued into the new year and Harry Greenwood's turn came in March 1919. He was stationed at the Officers Dispersal Unit, London when he was released from military service on 12 March. Prior to this he had again been deputising for Brigadier-General Edwards at Brigade HQ in France.

When the last batch of troops had been demobilised and sent home, in March 1919, the 9th Battalion, King's Own Yorkshire Light Infantry was disbanded. As a service battalion, raised to answer the country's call to arms, this was always to be its fate. During the four and a half years since its formation 9th KOYLI had distinguished itself on the battlefields of the Western Front, and with its disbandment another fine fighting battalion passed into history.

A month after Harry left the army his wife Helena gave birth to their third daughter. The family had moved back to Essex, and Violet Cynthia Marion (known as Cynthia) was born on Tuesday 1 April at Albrightleigh, High Road, Buckhurst Hill. This was to be the family home for the next few years until Harry's work took him to Africa on a regular basis.

Harry Greenwood received his Victoria Cross, together with the Bar to his DSO, from HM King George V at an investiture ceremony at

Harry Greenwood receiving his Victoria Cross from King George V in the quadrangle of Buckingham Palace 8 May 1919. (photograph: Cynthia List)

Buckingham Palace on Thursday 8 May 1919. The King, wearing the uniform of a British Field Marshal, shook hands heartily with Greenwood and remarked to him that only eight other officers had previously received the two decorations together. One newspaper reported that the King had "motored up from Windsor" for the occasion. It was a pleasant sunny day and the investitures were made in the quadrangle of the Palace. A raised platform had been built for the ceremony so that all present could see the King make the awards.

Although by then he had left the army, Harry Greenwood had retained his acting rank of Lieutenant-Colonel and attended the investiture in the uniform of that rank, complete with riding boots and spurs. On his right lower sleeve he wore three small chevrons, denoting his length of service, and on his left lower sleeve two wound stripes - strips of gold braid, each two inches long. This was no doubt a new uniform as his clothing was said to have been "shot through on several occasions during the two days of the *(VC)* action." At the ceremony, beginning at 11.00 am, the King made over 350 different awards starting with the Victoria Cross and Harry Greenwood was the first recipient. Helena Greenwood did not accompany her husband to the Palace on this occasion. She had given birth to their daughter, Cynthia, the previous month and was at home resting.

Four other VC heroes also received their awards from the King at the same ceremony. They were:

CSM Thomas Caldwell, 12th Battalion The Royal Scots Fusiliers
CSM Martin Doyle, 1st Battalion Royal Munster Fusiliers
Sergeant John Daykins, 2/4th Battalion The York & Lancaster Regiment
Private James Towers, 2nd Battalion The Cameronians (Scottish Rifles)

Daykins had been awarded the Victoria Cross for bravery at Solesmes, less than five miles from Ovillers, a few days before Greenwood. CSM Doyle had also been awarded the Military Medal and received this at the same investiture. All four Victoria Cross awards were announced in *The London Gazette* in January 1919.

A group photograph of the five men who received their VCs from the King on 8 May 1919 shows Lieutenant-Colonel Greenwood standing erect with his hands clasped in front of his pristine uniform. In what was clearly a proud moment for everyone Greenwood, the senior man there, appears the proudest of them all.

The date of the action for which each man was awarded his Victoria Cross was engraved on the reverse of the decoration. Details of name, rank and regiment were engraved on the reverse of the suspension bar. When the Great War campaign medals were issued Harry Greenwood received the 1914-15 Star, the British War Medal and the Victory Medal. This trio of medals was known by veterans as 'Pip, Squeak and Wilfred.' A small bronze oak leaf emblem on the Victory Medal showed that he had been mentioned in despatches (MID) during the war. Only one emblem was worn

Victoria Cross presentations at Buckingham Palace 8 May 1919.
Left to right: Pte James Towers, CSM Thomas Caldwell, Lt. Col. Harry Greenwood,
CSM Martin Doyle, Sgt John Daykins.
(photograph: Cynthia List)

even when the recipient had been mentioned many times - as was the case with Greenwood. Recipients also received certificates confirming that they had been Mentioned in Despatches.

Anecdotal evidence suggests that he may also have received the French Croix de Guerre, although the medal is not with the VC and other gallantry awards held by the KOYLI Museum. The Croix de Guerre was introduced in April 1915 for "feats of combat against Germany and her allies" and it was not unusual for awards to be made to British servicemen. Searches through the indexes of *The London Gazette*, French Government records and the MoD have failed to confirm this foreign award. Enquiries regarding a Belgian Croix de Guerre have also proved unsuccessful. Greenwood made no mention of this award in his *Who's Who* entry and it is thought unlikely that he received it.

The Treaty of Versailles, the first of many peace treaties, was signed on 28 June 1919, and 19 July was designated 'Peace Day.' Throughout Great Britain events were organised to celebrate this historic occasion.

During the same year Sir Alfred Butt (1878-1962), a wealthy and patriotic benefactor, gave silver medallions to all living Victoria Cross holders. Butt was the managing director of the Theatre Royal, Drury Lane and also had a number of other theatres under his control. The medallions, inscribed "Sir Alfred Butt's invitation to VCs" on the obverse, were intended as a means of free entry for the holders to those theatres.

Each 'invitation' was personally inscribed on the reverse. The whereabouts of Harry Greenwood's Butt's medallion is not known.

Many accounts of the War were published in the early 1920s. One in particular, *The Times History of the War,* a multi-volume edition, contained a colourful description of how Harry Greenwood had won his Victoria Cross. It was based on the VC citation but included such vivid phrases as ... "rushed the post and killed the crew and so like magic cleared away the menace to his troops" and ... "after that brilliant achievement."

Lieutenant-Colonel H. Greenwood VC, DSO and Bar, MC pictured after the end of the First World War.
Photograph from The Bugle *courtesy of the Light Infantry Office (Yorkshire).*

Chapter Nine

The Inter-War Years

Lieutenant-Colonel Greenwood was much in demand after his visit to Buckingham Palace to receive his Victoria Cross. Later the same month he was entertained to dinner by the Thames Camping and Boating Association. Although he was not known to have had connections with either pursuit, the Association would have been pleased to be connected with him. He was also the guest at a banquet given by members of the West Essex Golf Club, where he was presented with a silver salver and life membership of the club. In a speech of thanks Harry Greenwood, a keen golfer, told a number of golfing anecdotes, some of which were reported by the *Tottenham and Edmonton Weekly Herald* in its edition of 23 May 1919:

> *Whilst out of the line near Arras some time ago the Colonel with some officers had made a small putting green. They had quite a lot of fun with it until one morning an orderly reported to him:*
> *"Sir, the Bosche has holed out in one with an 11 inch shell on your putting green," an anecdote that tickled the golfers. "The most amazing thing was," said the Colonel, "that the gun was not shooting at our green at all !"*
> *"I am afraid," he concluded, "there is very little I can do in return for all the honour you have done me tonight. But there is one thing that is within my power and that is to present the club with a souvenir of the war in the shape of a machine-gun, in the capture of which I had some share. I have a great sentimental regard for the gun since it was fired by a very brave man, nevertheless an enemy, and I would not part with it except to very great friends." Needless to say the offer was accepted with acclamation.*

West Essex Golf Club no longer has the machine-gun and does not know what happened to this unusual souvenir. It is most likely that it was melted down for the war effort during the Second World War. Since Lieutenant-Colonel Greenwood regularly captured German machine-guns it is difficult to say where that particular gun was picked up.

In 1920 King George V decided to host a garden party in recognition of the outstanding bravery and sacrifice of the surviving VC recipients of all wars. Harry Greenwood was pleased to accept the invitation to 'His Majesty's Garden Party to Recipients of the Victoria Cross' held in the grounds of Buckingham Palace on Saturday 26 June 1920. It was the first Victoria Cross reunion, and the largest gathering of VC recipients since the first investiture in Hyde Park in 1857.

Each VC recipient was allowed to bring up to two guests, and railway warrants for the train journey to and from London were provided. After lunch at Wellington Barracks, as guests of the Brigade of Guards, the VC holders assembled on the parade ground and marched to Buckingham Palace where they were entertained by the King and Queen. The march was arranged in groups according to service and regiment and the army, with the most VCs, formed the most number of groups. Greenwood was in Group Seven together with five other King's Own Yorkshire Light Infantry VC recipients. Marching four abreast they made their way to the Palace via Birdcage Walk, Horse Guards Parade and The Mall and were cheered as they passed the enthusiastic crowds that had come to see them.

When the procession, led by the Band of the Welsh Guards, arrived inside the gates of the Palace garden the columns halted. By then the relatives of the men, including Helena Greenwood, were already in the garden. The VC recipients were then re-marshalled on the lawn into new groups to be received by the King. There were seven groups (A-G) based on order of seniority of award. Harry Greenwood was in Group F, which included all the VCs awarded during the period January to November 1918. After the King had inspected the lines each VC recipient was presented to him in turn. The King shook hands with each man and said a few words to most of them. As one of the last VCs of the Great War, Harry Greenwood was number 287 in line to meet King George. The first to be presented was General Sir Dighton Probyn VC, Comptroller of Queen Alexandra's Household, who was 87 and won his VC during the Indian Mutiny.

The Times of 28 June 1920 reported that:

> *After the presentations had all been made, refreshments were served and many of the guests formed small parties on the lawn. Later the members of the Royal Family moved among them, with a lack of formality which surprised some of the visitors.*

Over 300 VC recipients attended the Garden Party and press and court photographers were on hand to record this historic event for posterity. Lieutenant-Colonel Greenwood, wearing his army uniform, can be seen in the background of a photograph of a group of VC naval officers at Wellington Barracks.

Later that year Greenwood was present at the unveiling of the Cenotaph, and also the interment of the Unknown Warrior. The funeral service was held in Westminster Abbey at 11.00 am on 11 November 1920, the second anniversary of the Armistice. The body of an unidentified British soldier who had died on the Western Front was selected by a blindfolded officer and brought back to England with a military escort. A gun-carriage bearing the coffin, with pall-bearers from all the services marching on either side of it, passed through the streets of London on its journey to the Abbey.

A face in the crowd. Lt. Col. Harry Greenwood VC at Wellington Barracks before the 1920 VC Garden Party at Buckingham Palace (see enlarged detail). The naval officers in the foreground are: (left to right) Lieutenants Percy Dean VC, Gordon Steele VC, Augustine Agar VC, Admiral of the Fleet Sir Arthur Wilson VC and Captain Eduard Unwin VC. (photograph: Imperial War Museum, Q66160)

Inside Westminster Abbey the coffin was carried through two lines of 100 men who had won the Victoria Cross or otherwise distinguished themselves during the war. Harry Greenwood was one of the 74 VC recipients forming the Guard. The VC Guard had assembled on the parade ground of Chelsea Barracks earlier that morning and marched to Westminster Abbey, arriving there at 10.00 am.

The Unknown Warrior was buried with full military honours to commemorate "the many multitudes who during the Great War of 1914-1918 gave the most a man can give, life itself." King George V, as chief mourner for the Empire, was present and stood at the foot of the coffin during the service. At the committal the King scattered soil brought from France over the coffin. The two lines of holders of the Victoria Cross filed past the grave after the 'Last Post' and 'Reveille' were sounded.

On the way to the Abbey the coffin containing the Unknown Warrior, with its VC Guard, stopped at the Cenotaph in Whitehall. The King placed a wreath at the foot of the monument and unveiled it as a permanent memorial to the dead of the Great War. In later years Harry and his wife Helena were often present at the Cenotaph on Armistice Day. They had seats in the Foreign Office with a good view of the ceremony. There must have been some influence exerted somewhere to obtain that privilege. Harry always wore his uniform, complete with medals, to these occasions and he received great respect from taxi drivers, many of them old soldiers, when they saw his Victoria Cross.

In November 1929 the Prince of Wales (later King Edward VIII) held a reunion dinner for VC holders at the House of Lords. 321 holders of the Victoria Cross attended the Dinner - more than had attended the first VC reunion in 1920. Harry Greenwood was invited but had to decline as by then he had returned to West Africa on business and was unable to attend.

After leaving the army, with his rank of Lieutenant-Colonel, Harry Greenwood VC DSO* MC rejoined Sir Robert Williams and Co, a company he had been connected with since 1901.

In the early 1920s he was sent to Africa as Commercial Manager of the Benguela Railway. The railway was named after the Benguela plateau, across which it wends its way, in the west of Angola (then Portuguese West Africa). Covering an area just over five times the size of the United Kingdom, Angola is a large country with a relatively small population, mostly living in rural communities. The Benguela Railway (Caminho de Ferro de Benguela) is still the most important line in the country.

Greenwood later became a director of several Williams Group Companies, including the Benguela Railway Co, Benguela Estates Ltd, Angola Estates Ltd and Zambesia Exploring Co Ltd. Most of these companies were based in the then Portuguese colony of Angola, and many are now owned by Société Générale de Belgique. In his role as Company Director Harry Greenwood made frequent and often lengthy trips to Africa and was considered a model ambassador of British enterprise. On one occasion *The Star* of Johannesburg commented that he had a "frank kindliness which in any international zone makes of the world one family."

*Harry Greenwood at the wedding of his brother John, July 1924.
Back row: (left to right) John, David, Harry
Front row: Kathleen Baker, Kitty, Margaret, Maria Baker, Helena, David (son of David).
(photograph: Mrs Patricia Roberts)*

From about 1924 onwards he spent approximately ten years in Portuguese West Africa, living in Lobito Bay on the Atlantic coast. Lobito is one of the best shipping ports in Africa and has a large deepwater harbour protected by a strip of sand that protrudes above water to form Lobito Bay. While there Greenwood was Resident Director for the Williams Group. He lived in style in modern accomodation and had a native servant called 'Branco.'

Though not formally trained as an engineer and, initially, possessing no great knowledge of the working of railway systems Harry Greenwood was, nonetheless, well qualified to be a director of the company. His previous army experience of man management and the logistics of moving vast supplies of equipment around the country proved to be of great benefit to his work in Africa. He could also call on the services of expert engineers and geologists when required, and demonstrated that he was capable of mastering any new situation.

Africa in the 1920s was an exciting place to be. The railways were opening up much of the interior previously unknown to the outside world and a director of a railway company would have had a certain amount of influence and power. Even this position, however, would still have been an anti-climax after the thrill of commanding an infantry battalion in France during the war.

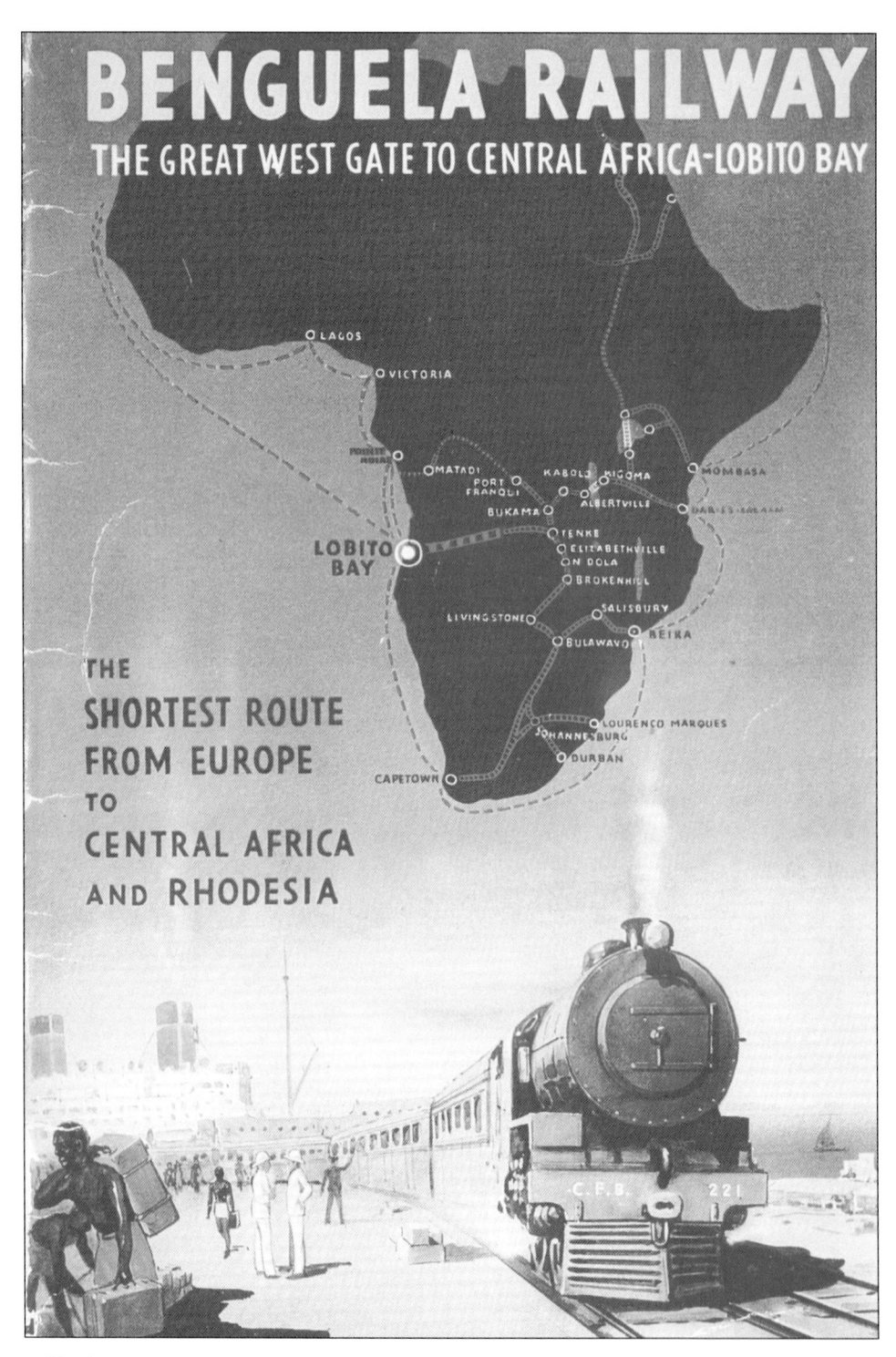

The front cover of a promotional booklet for the Benguela Railway. During the inter-war years Harry Greenwood was the resident director of the railway at Lobito Bay.

The Benguela Railway - "the Great West Gate to Central Africa"- was the showpiece of all the Williams Group Companies. It was 837 miles long, built to the Standard African Gauge of 3 ft 6 in, and ran from Lobito Bay on the Atlantic coast to the eastern frontier of Angola. There it adjoined the Belgian Congo (now the Democratic Republic of Congo) and linked up with most of central and southern Africa. The railway was conceived and built by Williams to enable the mineral wealth of central Africa, particularly the vast copper resources of the Katanga district of the Congo, to be transported to Europe. Williams was a great pioneer in the opening up of central Africa and helped develop the mining industries in those areas in which he had interests. Building of the Benguela Railway began in 1903 but was held up by the Great War and further delayed by postwar financial difficulties. With the help of British Government funds the railway reached the Angola-Congo border by 1928 and in March 1931 the route from Lobito Bay to the line leading to the Cape was completed.

Cynthia Greenwood, Harry's youngest daughter, was later to recall:

Prince George (later Duke of Kent) came out to officially open the railway - quite an excitement of course - as we were in Lobito at the time and due to return to England. We all sailed home on the same ship, the RMS Windsor Castle.

Harry Greenwood's visits were often reported in the African newspapers of the time. *The Star* of Johannesburg noted in November 1932:

Colonel Harry Greenwood VC who arrived at Lobito Bay in the Ubena, has, since 1901, been associated with Sir Robert Williams. He expects to be a year in Africa. Colonel Greenwood has had an extraordinary career. The son of a soldier, he himself would have chosen the army had circumstances permitted. At seventeen and a half (sic) *he came to South Africa with the CIV, served through the campaign, and it was shortly afterwards that his association with Sir Robert Williams's enterprises began. In the Great War his courage and his good fortune were remarkable. He won the VC, a double DSO, the Croix de Guerre and a Military Cross, and several Mentions in Despatches.*

This is the only contemporary newspaper report seen to suggest that Greenwood may have been awarded the Croix de Guerre, and may be based on a misquote. He certainly deserved this foreign award, but there is no evidence that he received it.

A *Bulawayo Chronicle* correspondent reported in *African World* in April 1935:

Colonel H. Greenwood VC DSO MC, representing Sir Robert Williams, who accompanied Earl Grey, a director of Tanganyika

Concessions, from Lobito Bay as far as Broken Hill was an interested visitor to Ndola this week... Up to the time of the Great War Colonel Greenwood was private secretary to Sir Robert Williams, when he immediately joined up, and was one of the first to receive the VC (sic). *It is over nine years since Colonel Greenwood last saw Ndola, and he was astounded to note the progress that the town has made.*

When asked about traffic on the railways between Ndola and Lobito Bay he spoke very enthusiastically and said that both passenger and goods traffic were steadily increasing, and there was no doubt that Lobito Bay was the coming port for Northern Rhodesia and many places in Southern Rhodesia... He felt sure immediately the Belgian Congo railway rates were reduced nothing could prevent all traffic for Northern Rhodesia coming over the Benguela Railways.

During the 1930s the Benguela Railway produced a booklet promoting the railway, in which Harry Greenwood was pictured looking out the window of one of the first class railway coaches. He was also shown with "a group of tourists at the entrance of the bridge over the River Cuanza." Sir Robert and Lady Williams were also in the picture.

Williams was by no means racist, but in keeping with the times the railway published the following information for passengers:

Natives, if properly dressed in European clothes, may be allowed to travel in the superior classes. Native servants, clean and properly dressed, may accompany their masters in the coaches or reserved compartments, on payment of the fare for the class of carriage in which they travel.

After his final return from Africa in the mid 1930s Greenwood worked at the Head Office of Sir Robert Williams & Co in Gresham Street, in the City of London. He continued to work there until the beginning of the Second World War. The England that Greenwood returned to was a changed one, with the worldwide depression still causing mass unemployment and rising inflation. There was also a very real fear of a further war as fascism took hold in Europe.

Robert Williams had been created a Baronet in 1928 in recognition of his work during the previous half century in the development of Africa. He also received Belgian and Portuguese honours and was an honorary LL.D. of Aberdeen University. As Sir Robert Williams of Park, Co Aberdeen and of Livingstone, Northern Rhodesia he lived in retirement in Aberdeen, where he died, aged 78, on 25 April 1938.

The Bishop of Aberdeen and Orkney gave the address at the funeral service, which was held in the West Church of St Nicholas, Aberdeen on 28 April. Williams was considered important enough for Prince Arthur of Connaught to send a representative to what was essentially a family

TYPE OF FIRST CLASS COACH ON THE BENGUELA RAILWAY

*Illustration from the Benguela Railway booklet.
Harry Greenwood is looking out of the railway carriage.*

*Illustration from the Benguela Railway booklet.
Harry Greenwood (arrowed) with a group of tourists.*

funeral. Kitty Greenwood attended with Williams's daughters and other family members. The burial took place privately in Drumoak Churchyard, Aberdeenshire.

A separate memorial service at Holy Trinity, Brompton in London the same day was attended by, *inter alia,* the Belgian Ambassador and the South African and Southern Rhodesian High Commissioners. The Duke of Kent and Prince Arthur of Connaught sent representatives and Princess Arthur of Connaught attended. Harry Greenwood went to the memorial service and was listed in *The Times* as "among others present at the service," along with representatives from many of Williams's companies.

In September of the same year Britain averted another world war when the Prime Minister, Neville Chamberlain, met Adolf Hitler at Munich. With other European leaders Chamberlain signed away the rights of Czechoslovakia and declared back home that he had secured "peace in our time." The inevitable showdown with the German dictator was merely postponed for a year.

During the First World War Harry Greenwood's younger sister Kate (known as Kitty or Kit) had replaced him as Sir Robert's private secretary - a position she was determined to retain. The war had seen the emergence of women workers into previously male areas of employment, including commerce. Not all had achieved such highly responsible positions, however, and as Sir Robert's assistant, Kitty had helped him run his companies. She would not have welcomed relinquishing this power on the return from war of her older brother.

Kitty and Robert Williams became close friends. Williams had married in 1886 and he and his wife had three children, a son who was killed in the war and two daughters. Kitty Greenwood never married. When Williams died in 1938 he left Kitty a generous legacy in money and shares, enabling her to retire and move to Scotland. Prior to that she had lived in a flat in Earl's Terrace, Kensington in London. On retirement she rented a former farmhouse, owned by a distant cousin on the Abernethy side of the family, just outside the village of Kellas-by-Elgin in Morayshire (now Grampian). The house was named 'Brokentore' and had its own trout lake.

Kitty's dominant nature can be seen in the photograph of the Greenwood family leaving Buckingham Palace after Harry had received his DSO in July 1918. Most people would assume that the woman walking alongside Harry and daughter Mollie is his wife, Helena. Not so. It is Kitty, and Helena is walking slightly behind the others carrying the child's coat. Kitty was held in great awe by the Greenwood family until her death in the 1950s.

Both Harry's parents died in the 1920s, within a short time of each other. His mother died first, on 30 August 1926 aged 71, and his father less than eight months later. Margaret was in a nursing home in Ponders End, London at the time of her death. She bequeathed her entire estate, with a gross value of £737-0s-2d, (in excess of £20,000 in today's money) to her daughter Kitty. Charles Greenwood died in the North Middlesex Hospital, following a short illness, on 8 April 1927 aged 73. He had not retired and had kept working until shortly before his death. His occupation was officially described as "Yeoman, Royal Bodyguard of the King's Yeoman of the Guard." In his will, written the day after his wife died, Charles bequeathed everything to all his children in equal shares.

Margaret and Charles were buried in Tottenham Cemetery in the same family plot where their youngest daughter Mary Ann, who died as a teenager, and Harry Greenwood's infant son were also buried. Further brief inscriptions were added to the plinths beneath the cross to record their passing away. In the case of Margaret Greenwood a line of remembrance was also added: "He giveth his beloved sleep." Harry's younger brother Arthur, who died in 1965, is also buried in the cemetery.

Mollie Greenwood, the oldest of Harry's daughters, returned to Angola with her father in 1931. There she met her future husband, a Portuguese young man working locally. After the wedding they lived at Mossamedes, down the coast. Sadly, Mollie died at an early age less than a year after marriage. In 1933, while in a weakened condition during childbirth, she contracted Blackwater Fever, a serious complication of malaria. She died, aged 19, and was buried in Angola. This was an especially heavy blow for Harry and Helena as Mollie was the second of their four children to die young.

Prior to Harry and Mollie returning to Africa in 1931 the Greenwood family lived in Dulwich Village, London. Evelyn and Cynthia, together with their mother, then spent a year in Switzerland in 1934 to assist their education before moving to Wimbledon.

The Greenwood family settled in Wimbledon, SW London in the mid 1930s. In 1935 they moved to 77 Home Park Road, Wimbledon Park, part of a newly built development overlooking Wimbledon Golf Course. This must have been a very attractive location for Harry who listed golf, as well as shooting, as his main recreations in *Who's Who*. He never showed much enthusiasm for football, even though Wimbledon had its own football team.

Although he had become a relatively wealthy man through his business work in Africa he did not own the house. Home ownership was not as widespread in the 1930s as it is today so Harry Greenwood would not have thought it unusual to rent the property. He is first listed as living at this address in *Kelly's Directory* for 1936 so must have moved there mid to late 1935.

The move to Wimbledon Park, an up-market part of Wimbledon, was probably prompted by a desire for the two girls, unlike their father, to have some form of formal education. Evelyn and Cynthia both attended Wimbledon High School. The large detached house in Home Park Road is still there, although it is now divided into three separate flats. There is, at present, no plaque there to record the fact that it is the former home of Lieutenant-Colonel Harry Greenwood VC. In 2001 the London Borough of Merton made an official request for a plaque to English Heritage, but this was turned down. The Blue Plaques Panel "were mindful of the very small number of plaques that English Heritage can erect each year" and took account of "other figures already commemorated, including First Viscount

*Two views of Harry Greenwood's home at 77 Home Park Road, Wimbledon.
(photographs: Derek Hunt)*

Allenby and Field Marshal Viscount Montgomery." (Neither of them had Wimbledon connections.)

Harry and his family often went on holiday with his brother Arthur and his family. A favourite holiday resort was Bexhill-on-Sea, East Sussex, where both families stayed at a house on the seafront. Both Harry and Arthur were keen golfers and became members of the local Cooden Beach Golf Club, which was close to their holiday home. One of Harry's nephews, John Greenwood, remembers those holidays with great affection:

> *It was Harry's habit to spend the morning on the golf course, to return to the house for lunch, then, after a suitable interval for digestion, weather and tide permitting, to supervise a family bathe. We always knew when he had played a bad game of golf because he would arrive back from Cooden with a "brow as black as thunder," and would only utter growling answers to greetings. He would take lunch in morose silence, after which he would go into the garden and stick a row of matchsticks into the ground. He would then spend some time swinging at them with a golf club until he could hit them cleanly every swing.*
>
> *When he was satisfied, he would come back into the house full of smiles and good temper and would marshal all the children present (his own family, our family and any other spare children we had managed to befriend on the beach) for a bathing parade. He was extremely good and careful to see that no child got into difficulties, and encouraged us all to improve our swimming prowess. It was at that time he taught me to dive, and although I loved swimming, I had never fancied the idea of plunging head first into the water. Harry used to stand in about five feet of water and get me to climb on to his shoulders where I stood while he held me steady. He then would give me a little shove and I would take a header into the sea. I have never since then had any fear of diving into water. I can remember many kindnesses my brother (Charles) and I received from Harry, and looking back I believe that much of this came from the fact that he had three daughters and looked upon us as the sons he never had.*

Harry Greenwood was a great sportsman and later in life, when he was in his mid fifties, decided to take up skiing. In about 1936 he took his family for a winter sports holiday to Wengen in the Bernese Oberland. There he approached the challenge with his customary enthusiasm. Never having been on skis before, he was advised to start on the nursery slopes in a class under an instructor. He found this rather slow, however, and next day he took the railway up to the beginning of one of the steep ski-runs. He then put on his skis and proceeded to ski down the mountain. Unfortunately, he was not entirely successful and later picked himself up in the valley below with two cracked ribs. He got a local doctor to strap him up in plaster and the next day was back on the ski-slopes. Such behaviour is typical of Greenwood's response to rise to the next challenge.

Having tried skiing he became keen on ice skating, in the short period leading up to the outbreak of war in 1939. He used to spend Sunday afternoons at the Westminster Ice Club, London, with his family and nephews and their young friends. This fairly large party, all skating enthusiastically, was genially presided over by Harry who tried to match them. He never became a particularly good skater himself though, being a little too old for much more than a gentle amble round the rink. He was, nonetheless, greatly loved and admired by those he took on these outings. Harry was always keen to take the lead in these circumstances. He was a generous and gregarious man who tried to enjoy life to the full.

He also had a keen interest in boxing, though as a spectator not a competitor, and was a member of the National Sporting Club (NSC). The club used to hold regular evening events at which promising young boxers had the opportunity of sporting bouts in front of managers, promoters and enthusiasts of the sport. These were black tie affairs, and Harry and his brother Arthur often went off to the NSC for an evening of good boxing and returned with tales of the exciting bouts they had witnessed and how certain young hopefuls looked like going a long way in the ring.

While in Africa he had enjoyed his other sporting passion, shooting. He made the most of the opportunities available to him and often went 'big game' hunting.

Harry Greenwood had wide ranging tastes, and was also very fond of the theatre. He often took one of his younger brothers or sisters with him to such productions as *Bitter Sweet* and *Me and My Girl*. He liked the cinema, particularly Edward G. Robinson films.

During the late 1930s John and Charles Greenwood frequently spent weekends at Wimbledon with Uncle Harry and family. Very early on Sunday mornings he would take the two teenagers out in his Humber Snipe and teach them to drive. The Kingston By-Pass, the favoured training ground, was more or less deserted at that time of the morning and certainly carried a lot less traffic than it does today. He was surprisingly patient with his pupils for a man of sudden and fierce temper.

John Greenwood remembers his Uncle Harry as a very good and generous host who loved entertaining:

> *I shall always remember a party he gave at the Savoy Hotel in July 1938 to celebrate the 21st birthday of his daughter Evelyn. It was a very 'slap up' affair with plenty of champagne. In those days the dance music was provided by Geraldo and his Orchestra alternating with Carrol Gibbons and the Savoy Orpheans. They each played for half the evening. At a certain point during the first half, when Geraldo's band was in full swing, we noticed that Harry had left our table. A few moments later we were somewhat embarrassed to see him emerge on stage and appear to 'conduct' the orchestra. Geraldo, evidently a sportsman, discreetly retired to the side of the stage and continued to conduct unobtrusively, leaving Harry to his performance centre stage, to the applause of the audience.*

Fortunately Harry, flushed with success, soon left the stage, to the relief of his family. Later on when Carrol Gibbons had taken over, Harry, encouraged by his former success, tried his act on again, without the approval of Carrol Gibbons who was definitely not amused! Fortunately Gibbons led his band from the piano, so that he was not in a position to throw Harry off the stage and had to confine himself to sotto voce imprecations and expressions of disapproval. Harry, realising that the act was not going down as well as before, left the stage in good order, again to the relief of his embarrassed family.

The Savoy was Harry Greenwood's favourite spot for entertaining. During the First World War he had liked to entertain any member of the family who happened to be on leave in London at the same time as himself. He was a member of the Devonshire Club in St James's Street, London and would also take guests to lunch there.

Greenwood, and all other living holders of the Victoria Cross, received the Coronation Medal 1937 to celebrate the crowning of King George VI on 12 May 1937. He did not, however, receive the Jubilee Medal 1935 to celebrate the Silver Jubilee of King George V. This is confirmed by reference to the medal rolls held at the National Archives. No VC holder received the Jubilee Medal purely as a VC holder, whereas they all received the Coronation Medal in that capacity. Although not entitled to the Jubilee Medal, Greenwood, for whatever reason, wore the ribbon on his Pioneer Corps uniform during the Second World War (see photograph on page 116).

The post-war years, though very active as he travelled between England and Africa pursuing his business interests, allowed Greenwood to enjoy life to the full and take on more new challenges. He would have been dismayed as he saw the worsening situation in Europe in the late 1930s and the prospect of war looming yet again. All the death and destruction he had seen in "the war to end all wars" seemed likely to repeat itself.

Chapter Ten

Second World War

Britain was once again at war with Germany in September 1939. The humiliating peace terms imposed on Germany by the Treaty of Versailles had left a dangerous legacy of resentment. In the inter-war period nationalism and the worldwide depression had further led the way for the rise of political extremism. Adolf Hitler, leader of the right wing Nazi party, became Chancellor of Germany in January 1933 and embarked on a policy of re-building the country's armed forces and overturning the terms of the Versailles Treaty. The League of Nations did little to stop him. He occupied the demilitarised Rhineland, without opposition, and in March 1938 forced a union with Germany on Austria. Britain and France gave into Hitler's demands to govern the Sudetenland area of Czechoslovakia in September 1938 and took no action when Germany occupied the remaining parts of the country in March 1939. In Britain the fear of another European war as costly in lives as the previous one drove the Government's policy of appeasement. But such a policy could not ignore all of Hitler's territorial ambitions.

On 1 September 1939 German forces invaded Poland, a country which Britain had agreed to assist in the event of attack. The British Government, led by Neville Chamberlain, was determined to honour its obligations and advised the German Government that unless it withdrew its troops from Poland a state of war would exist. When this ultimatum was not met by the deadline of 11.00 am on Sunday 3 September 1939 Britain and, later the same day, France declared war on Germany.

Unlike 1914 the prospect of war was received with great apprehension in Britain. A British Expeditionary Force was sent to France but neither country was in a position to give practical assistance to Poland. Allied policy concentrated on protecting the French border against an expected German attack. However, when the attack finally came in May 1940 the heavily protected Maginot Line proved useless. The German Army had repeated the 1914 'Schlieffen Plan' by invading via Belgium and bypassing the French defence systems. Chamberlain resigned after losing a vote of confidence in the House of Commons and Winston Churchill became Prime Minister and formed a War Cabinet.

After the occupation of France and the withdrawal of the British Army at Dunkirk a German invasion of England looked likely. Coastal defences were strengthened and a Home Guard formed, but it was the decisive aerial fighting of the Battle of Britain (July - October 1940) which prevented an invasion. Against all odds the fighter pilots of the RAF defeated the might of the Luftwaffe.

As in the previous war Harry Greenwood was eager to serve his country and volunteered to join the army. This time, however, he was considered too old for active service. He was 57 when the war began.

He served instead in a UK based unit where his leadership skills and organising abilities were to prove just as useful to the war effort. On 15 February 1940, during the 'phoney war' period, Greenwood was enrolled into the Army Officers Emergency Reserve while a suitable job was found for his talents. He was appointed to an Emergency Commission as Lieutenant on 4 July, and on the following day was appointed Acting Lieutenant-Colonel (the rank he held at the end of the last war) and posted to No. 12 Pioneer Corps Centre as Commanding Officer. He was appointed War Substantive Major and Temporary Lieutenant-Colonel on 5 October 1940.

Officers did not have army numbers during the First World War, but from the early 1920s onwards they were allocated personal numbers, or 'P' numbers for short. Greenwood's personal number on rejoining the army was P/141511.

The Auxiliary Military Pioneer Corps had been raised in 1939, changing its name to The Pioneer Corps in 1940. (It did not receive the 'Royal' prefix until 1946.) Further training centres were established to meet the expected inflow of recruits and No. 12 Centre was the last to be formed. It was also the largest, and was established in June 1940 with its headquarters in a large requisitioned school in Dingle Vale, Liverpool. The centre took its first intake of civilians in July 1940 and the new recruits were given four weeks basic military training.

From August 1940 onwards the area was the target of concentrated German air raids. Liverpool, as well as London, suffered heavy attacks during the Blitz as the German bombers tried to destroy the city and its crucial dockyards. The intensity of the air raids decreased in May 1941 when the Luftwaffe began moving its bombers eastwards for the invasion of Russia. A raid over Liverpool in September 1940 hit several requisitioned buildings, and a working party from No. 12 Centre was sent to assist rescuers. The Centre itself was damaged slightly by a 'near miss' in December. Lieutenant-Colonel Greenwood frequently sent working and rescue parties out to assist the City Council restore public services following air raids. On 7 May 1941 Dingle Vale School received a direct hit, blowing out all the windows and doors and causing some structural damage. These wrecked premises were urgntly required by Liverpool Education Authority to replace other more badly damaged schools.

The same month the Centre was relocated to Pheasey Farm Estate in Great Barr, Birmingham. The Headquarters occupied the community recreational centre of the large slum clearance housing estate and the Training Companies were accommodated in the houses of the estate.

Between June 1940 and October 1945 No. 12 Centre was responsible for the training, documentation, kitting out and medical examination of over 124,000 recruits. Included in the Corps were 'friendly aliens,' conscientious objectors and other non-combatants. There were, naturally, some misgivings at the time about accepting and arming men from enemy countries. It was felt that their reliability was doubtful at best, but many of them served with distinction in The Pioneer Corps. At the time the Corps gained an unfair reputation for taking men that no other unit would have.

The Corps provided valuable assistance to the civilian authorities in loading and unloading ships' cargoes at Liverpool Docks, assisting the railway companies to deliver military equipment and helping to bring in the harvest in areas where there was a shortage of labour. The Pioneer Corps also helped other regiments and corps to carry out building projects in their own camps.

Though not employed in the front line Greenwood supplied men for a number of dangerous jobs, such as demolition and rescue work following enemy air raids, particularly in Liverpool when No. 12 Centre was based there.

The Pioneer, the Regimental magazine of The Pioneer Corps, recorded in a history of No. 12 Centre:

The Centre was commended by the Brigadier Commanding, Mersey Garrison, for its work in the blitzed city of Liverpool, and Colonel Greenwood received the personal thanks, both privately and in public, of the local councils of Bootle, Wallasey, Birkenhead, and Liverpool City itself in respect of the assistance the centre had rendered.

Another important task was the training and provision of cooks for units of The Pioneer Corps, both at home and overseas, and the supply of cooks for other training units. When they were fully trained personnel were also sent to Salvage Units, Smokescreen Units, Airfield Construction Units, Provost Units and other specialist Pioneer Corps formations.

In a report written after the war Lieutenant-Colonel Greenwood described the work of No. 12 Centre in relation to officers:

On arrival all officers report to the administration office, where they are documented and entries recorded on the card index... It (No. 12 Centre) *deals with the promotion and relinquishment of acting and temporary rank, relegation to unemployment, all questions of pay and allowances, issuing ration cards, warrants, new identity cards, etc.*

The Greenwood family had moved out of their Wimbledon home at the beginning of the war. Helena and Evelyn moved to a flat elsewhere, while Cynthia joined the First Aid Nursing Yeomanry (FANY). She later transferred to the Auxiliary Territorial Service (ATS) as she thought there would be more action in that unit and was stationed in various places, including Liverpool and London. Evelyn also joined the ATS and was stationed in Northern Ireland, where she had friends, and later in the north of England. They both chose driving jobs, and often drove ambulances, as neither wanted a routine office job.

Evelyn, known as Evie to her family, was once detailed to drive an officer to Harry Greenwood's Pioneer Camp when it was based at Oldham. During the journey the officer made a nuisance of himself with his unwanted attention. When they arrived at Oldham and Evelyn had got rid of her troublesome passenger, she went to the CO's office and asked to see her father. Harry was delighted by Evelyn's surprise visit and while they were catching up with family news a new officer to the camp was announced. To Evelyn's amusement her recent passenger was shown in. He recognised her and looked extremely embarrassed when Harry introduced her as his daughter. As *Punch* might have commented: "Complete collapse of amorous officer!"

Helena Greenwood, who was almost four years older than Harry, was 61 at the beginning of the war and was excused war service. Harry's sister Kitty became a Red Cross voluntary worker.

Many of Harry's brothers served during the Second World War. Arthur was recalled from the Emergency Reserve of Officers in September 1939. He joined a reserve regiment, with the rank of captain, training conscripts. He later attended a gunnery staff training course at the School of Artillery and qualified as an instructor in gunnery. Promoted to major, Arthur was transferred to the Army Welfare Service in 1943, and served in India until 1945.

David, who had joined the Indian Prison Service at the end of the previous war, served as a quartermaster with the Madras Guards, an Indian Territorial unit. John also spent the war years in India. He had been badly wounded in the First World War, which precluded him from active service. Charles remained in Canada with the Toronto Police. He retired in the 1950s with the rank of Inspector and died in 1968 aged 81.

Whenever he was on leave Harry Greenwood would return to The Savoy, in London, which had been his favourite venue for entertaining during the previous war. He would often meet members of the family there, when their own leave permitted, and was a generous host.

In April 1941 Greenwood was called as a witness in the Court Martial at Liverpool of an officer and several NCOs of The Pioneer Corps accused of ill-treating conscientious objectors. After the introduction of compulsory military service during the First World War men could apply for exemption from call-up for a number of reasons. Anyone who applied on grounds of morality or religious faith was a 'conscientious objector.' Many were genuine in their beliefs that the taking of life was wrong but others were simply trying to evade military service and were imprisoned.

The Times of 3 April 1941 reported that:

> *Colonel H. Greenwood VC, Officer Commanding the Centre, said he had considerable experience of conscientious objectors in the last war. Everything had gone well until men who had served terms of imprisonment began to arrive. He saw the conscientious objectors at least half a dozen times every day and asked if they had any complaints. They said "no."*

In the case against one of his officers Greenwood was reported as saying:

Because Captain Wright was probably one of the best instructional officers in the Centre, he was detailed to the difficult and unpleasant job of being second-in-command at this conscientious objectors' Training Centre. It was in a great measure owing to him that the first hundred conscientious objectors were got to join combatant forces.

Captain Wright told the court that he thought it was his duty to suppress a mutiny, which took the form of a refusal to obey orders. He was found 'not guilty' of assault.

Gracie Fields, the Lancashire-born star of stage and screen, visited No. 12 Centre in the West Midlands in August 1941 as part of her countrywide tour entertaining munitions workers and military camps. She was welcomed to the camp by Lieutenant-Colonel Greenwood but is said to have declined his invitation to tea in order that she would not keep the troops waiting. The *Walsall Observer* reported that she received a "vociferous welcome not only from the soldiers but the wives, sweethearts and children who were present."

The Pioneer Corps in turn helped to entertain and fundraise in the local community. In January 1942 Greenwood loaned the services of the 12th Centre band, which led the Aldridge Warship Week parade in the West Midlands. It was the aim of the district to raise sufficient funds through National Savings to sponsor a ship and Aldridge was said to be "on the warpath for a warship." Greenwood also arranged for the Pioneers' Dance Band to perform at a Warship Week dance at Great Barr the following week.

With the formation of the General Service Corps in February 1942, the Centres started to receive partly trained soldiers from the new corps. By then the USA had joined the war and large numbers of American troops started to arrive in England. The Americans soon requisitioned many buildings across the country, regardless of their existing use. Pheasey Farm Estate was allocated to the American Army and in June 1942 No. 12 Centre moved to Oldham and the surrounding districts. Finally, in July 1943, the Centre moved to the L.M.S. holiday camp in Prestatyn, north Wales, where it remained for the rest of the war. This sizeable accommodation consisting of chalets, huts, offices and other buildings of the well-appointed pre-war holiday camp meant that for the first time in years all the various units of No. 12 Centre were brought together in one place.

Eventually all the other Pioneer Corps Centres were merged under the overall command of Lieutenant-Colonel Greenwood. His unit, comprising almost 7,000 men of all ranks, was responsible for the entire administrative work of the Corps.

The Pioneer later recorded:

The more completely centralised administrative control made possible by the more compact form the Centre has assumed made the re-

*Lieutenant-Colonel Greenwood in Pioneer Corps uniform 1944.
He is wearing the following medals:
First row: Victoria Cross, DSO and Bar, MC, Queen's South Africa Medal
Second row: King's South Africa Medal, 1914-15 Star, British War Medal
1914-20, Victory Medal
Third row: 1935 Jubilee Medal, 1937 Coronation Medal.
(photograph: Cynthia List)*

organisation then so necessary much simpler to achieve. Colonel Greenwood therefore made the necessary plans for the complete re-organisation of the central administration, the suggested plans being submitted to the War Office and finally approved in July 1944. The unit was thenceforward known as No. 12 Pioneer Corps Holding and Training Unit...

His tireless work in the re-organisation of The Pioneer Corps was rewarded with his appointment as an Officer of the Military Division of the Most Excellent Order of the British Empire (OBE). The Order of the British Empire had been founded in 1917 to reward services to the Empire at home and overseas. A Military Division was added the following year. The award was announced in the King's Birthday Honours List and recorded in a supplement dated 8 June to *The London Gazette* of 2 June 1944. It showed Greenwood's rank as "Major (Temporary Lieutenant-Colonel)."

Many Pioneer Corps units had been posted overseas. Lord Mountbatten stated that without the assistance of The Pioneer Corps the work of his South East Asia Command could not have been completed. Other Pioneer units had taken part in the D-Day invasion and later distinguished themselves at Caen and Nijmegen. The successful crossing of the Rhine was due in part to the smoke screen The Pioneer Corps put up to conceal Allied preparations.

Greenwood was keen to see action again and requested that he be allowed to take a unit over to Normandy to support the fighting troops on D-Day in June 1944. This offer was declined, however, in view of his age as he was then 62 years old. Though disappointed he already knew that his active service days were over. Greenwood remained in the UK throughout the war. He was later quoted as saying of the men of his Corps:

When trouble came they were too old to run away. They fought with what they had where they were. And usually they were never heard of again.

In January 1945 recommendations were forwarded to the War Office that with the increased size of No. 12 Holding and Training Unit and Lieutenant-Colonel Greenwood now commanding in excess of 5,000 men he be promoted to the rank of full Colonel. This was carried out six months later with an 'Acting' promotion.

Russia had joined the war when German forces invaded without warning in June 1941, and America was reluctantly brought into the conflict in December that year when Japan attacked the American Fleet at Pearl Harbor. After D-Day Germany found itself fighting on two fronts a war it could not win. The war in Europe ended in May 1945, and 8 May was declared Victory in Europe (VE) Day. Hitler had committed suicide at the end of April and the victorious Allied armies overran the defeated Germany. The war in the Pacific, however, was to last another three months before the surrender of Japan.

Unlike the active combat units, the Holding and Training Units of The Pioneer Corps did not maintain daily War Diaries. Shortly after VE-Day Colonel C. J. Scott, the Directorate of Labour at the War Office, wrote to Lieutenant-Colonel Greenwood requesting details of the history of the unit since its formation in June 1940. Greenwood replied in a memo dated 20 May enclosing two foolscap pages of reports and a further three pages of appendices. He added:

I take it you do not want me to go to any great lengths with this, so have compressed it as much as possible to give a concise picture of our organisation and work here.

The record of work done was impressive. The total turnover of Pioneer Corps and non-combatant corps at No. 12 Centre/Unit was 234,597. Greenwood broke this down as total intake 120,163 and total output 114,434. Over 11,000 officers were processed, with the average number of officers at the Centre/Unit being 350.

A complete history of No. 12 Centre/Unit was also provided, from its formation in Liverpool in 1940 until the end of the War, giving dates and details of all the changes of location and organisation.

Although the Second World War was over Greenwood was to remain in the army for another year. He was appointed Acting Colonel in The Pioneer

HEADQUARTERS STAFF (OFFICERS) OF No. 12 PIONEER CORPS H. & T. UNIT.

Back Row:
Capt. C. C. Williams, Lieut. S. C. Louis, Lieut. F. C. Stevens, Lieut. F. S. Dove, M.M., Capt. J. Smith, Capt. J. E. Francis (A.C.C), Capt. B. S. Hawkins, Capt. H. Langham.
Middle Row:
Capt. J. H. Crocker, Capt. R. N. O. Moynan (R.A.M.C.), Capt. P. Knight, Capt. R. F. Smallwood, Capt. E. Cutts (R.A.M.C.), Major F. J. Manning R.A.M.C.), Rev. D. D. Thomas (R.A.Ch.D.), Capt. L. S. Turnpenny, Capt. P. Honan (R.A.M.C.), Capt. W. H. A. Perry.
Front Row:
Jnr. Comdr. E. M. Edwards (A.T.S.), Major A. T. White, Major F. H. McKay, Lt.-Col. H. M. E. Flateau, Col. H. Greenwood, V.C., D.S.O., O.B.E., M.C., Capt. H. E. Parsons, M.C., Major W. Warwick, Major H. E. Miller, Major H. W. Dunster, Sub. L. Searby, (A.T.S.).

Photograph from The Pioneer *courtesy of The Royal Logistic Corps*

Colonel H. Greenwood, V.C., D.S.O., O.B.E., M.C.
Commander No. 12 Pioneer Corps H. & T. Unit.

Photograph from The Pioneer *courtesy of The Royal Logistic Corps.*

Corps on 6 July 1945 and then Temporary Colonel on 6 January 1946, with the War Substantive rank of Lieutenant-Colonel. Demobilisation started as soon as the war had ended but such a huge task took time to fully implement.

Chapter Eleven

Post War Years

When campaign medals were awarded after the war Harry Greenwood was entitled to two medals. Although he had not served overseas his service with The Pioneer Corps in the UK had earned him the Defence Medal and the War Medal 1939-1945. These medals had to be claimed by the recipient or next-of-kin and were not awarded automatically, or named, like the campaign medals of the previous war. Greenwood, however, never claimed his entitlement of Second World War medals. By then his health was deteriorating and there were many more pressing demands on his time. The Ministry of Defence still holds these medals, as it does for thousands of other ex-servicemen, and up to the end of 2002 they had not been claimed by his family (see Appendix I for full list of medals awarded).

During the lengthy process of demobilisation Harry Greenwood relinquished his appointment as Officer Commanding No. 12 Pioneer Corps Holding and Training Unit, though not his rank of Temporary Colonel, on 3 June 1946.

A Victory Parade was held in London on Saturday 8 June 1946, exactly one year and one month after VE-Day. The date was chosen to give as many people as possible the chance to come to the capital to see the Victory celebrations. Monday 10 June was Whitsun Bank Holiday, allowing sightseers time to make their way home before returning to work. Contingents from all the victorious Allied forces, together with the Royal Navy, the RAF and every British regiment marched from Marble Arch to Hyde Park Corner. There was also a mechanised procession and The King took the salute as the combined columns passed up The Mall. The Pioneer Corps marched, with other corps and services of the British Army, behind the infantry of the line regiments. Many of the Victoria Cross winners who were present travelled together in a group rather than with their former units. Colonel Greenwood, still a serving officer, was to have taken part in the parade but ill-health intervened.

On the day before the parade he was suddenly taken ill with severe abdominal pains. After being examined by his doctor he was admitted, as an emergency case, into the Nelson Memorial Hospital in Merton, Surrey near his home in Wimbledon. He was diagnosed as suffering from an intestinal obstruction and operated on the same day - Friday 7 June. Harry Greenwood was naturally very annoyed at not being able to take part in the Victory Parade. He had earned his place there but was not in any fit state for marching.

A second operation was performed on 6 July for carcinoma of the sigmoid colon (bowel cancer) and a tumour removed, but by then the cancer had already taken hold. Although he recovered from the operation this illness was eventually to lead to his premature death. Harry Greenwood was discharged from the Nelson Hospital on 30 July 1946. He was never to regain his robust health and his gradual decline was a sad ending for a man who had always been so active.

Colonel Greenwood is said to have been present at the dinner for Victoria Cross recipients at The Dorchester, London (where another Victoria Cross recipient, Oliver Brooks, was doorman during the 1930s) on the evening of the Victory Parade. *The News of the World*, which organised and paid for the event, published a list of all the VC guests in its edition of Sunday 9 June 1946. Harry Greenwood VC was listed, but although invited he was unable to attend as he was in hospital at the time.

He relinquished his Temporary rank of Colonel on 3 October 1946. In view of his continuing ill health he relinquished his commission on 16 May 1947 and formally left the army. He was granted the honorary rank of Colonel.

Harry and Helena Greenwood and their two daughters returned to the family home at Home Park Road, Wimbledon after the war. John Greenwood, together with his brother Charles, continued to visit his Uncle Harry and remembers the frequent family gatherings:

Sometimes Harry used to spring a surprise on us. One Saturday evening when we were invited to dinner Harry surprised us by singing a song for us, accompanied by his wife Helena. On another occasion he entertained us with a violin solo. We later learnt from his daughters that both performances had been rehearsed for a week beforehand. Harry certainly enjoyed being the centre of attention.

He took himself seriously and to those who did not know him well he may have seemed a bit of a 'show-off.' But there was nothing vain about Harry Greenwood. Such displays, which were meant to impress, were all part of his sense of fun and his love of life.

Despite failing health he took part in a number of regimental reunions. In October 1947 at a meeting of the London branch of the KOYLI Association he was pictured with two of the Regiment's other VC winners - Captain Frederick Holmes and Sergeant Laurence Calvert. His former regiment The King's Own Yorkshire Light Infantry (KOYLI) was merged in 1968 with several other Light Infantry regiments, including the Durham Light Infantry (DLI) which had served with KOYLI in 64th Infantry Brigade during the First World War. The new regiment became The Light Infantry.

Greenwood's daughters married after the war was over. Evelyn married Malcolm Brooks Onwood, then a Lieutenant in the 2nd Battalion Duke of Wellington's Regiment, at the Church of the Oratory, Brompton Road, London on 7 August 1946. Harry and Helena Greenwood both attended the wedding, and Harry recorded his occupation in the register as "Colonel, HM Army."

Part of the meeting of the London Branch, October, 1947.
Seated: Capt. F. Holmes, V.C., Sjt. L. Calvert, V.C. and Colonel H. Greenwood, V.C.

Photograph from The Bugle *courtesy of the Light Infantry Office (Yorkshire).*

Cynthia married Richard List at Wimbledon Parish Church on 1 May 1948. Harry was not well enough to attend the wedding, although Helena was there. In the absence of her father the bride was given away by her Uncle Arthur (Harry's younger brother), who signed the register as a witness to the marriage. The newlyweds returned from their honeymoon just days before Harry Greenwood's death.

Richard List had served in the Royal Corps of Signals during the war and was working for the Westminster Bank at the time he married Cynthia. Both daughters later emigrated to the USA with their husbands.

One of Cynthia's friends, Rosamond Nicholls, recalls how she first met the Greenwood family after the war:

In the summer of 1946 when I came out of the WAAF my parents took me to stay at the Burlington Hotel, Eastbourne for a holiday. While there we met up with the Greenwood family who, like us, were there with their daughters. Cynthia had also just left the forces and we became good friends. All of us had a most happy time.

The following April I got married to my first husband, Himley Cartwright, and Cynthia was one of my bridesmaids. Colonel and Mrs Greenwood came to the wedding and it was lovely having them. My husband's best man was Richard List and only a month or two afterwards Cynthia and Richard became engaged. Sadly, by then Cynthia's father was very unwell. He did not attend their wedding and died soon afterwards.

> *I remember Harry Greenwood as a very dear and jolly person and a most devoted family man. Once or twice he took us to The Savoy for lunch, a great treat, and we always had a wonderful time as he was especially friendly with the head waiter there.*

Continuing ill health was having an effect on his ability to entertain and be the centre of attention - though not on his sense of fun. John Greenwood recalls one such occasion:

> *Not long after the war, perhaps about 1947 or 1948, we had a lunch party in London with some of our Nottingham relations. Harry, unfortunately, was not able to be present. When my father afterwards described this affair to Harry, he sadly shook his head and remarked "Ah, Hamlet without the Prince of Denmark!"*

As the months of terminal illness wore on, Harry would have had ample opportunity to reflect upon his life and his achievements. He had served his country well in three wars, been a successful businessman with frequent trips to Africa and was blessed with a loving family. He had also been awarded the Victoria Cross and other gallantry awards, but he regarded these as having been won while performing his duty. Although he had received the Freedom of the City of London in 1900 it brought with it no financial benefits or privileges, other than the ancient right of being able to drive sheep across London Bridge - something Greenwood had never considered. There had been tragedies as well as triumphs, and the early deaths of his infant son Harry and his teenage daughter Mollie still grieved him. But all in all, it had been a good life.

He had known for some time that he was dying, but there would have been nothing that could be done apart from prescribing drugs to try and alleviate the pain. Radiotherapy had been in use as a treatment for cancer for decades, but was then not as refined in its application as it is today.

Harry Greenwood died after a long illness, borne in his usual courageous manner, at his home in Wimbledon on Wednesday 5 May 1948. The cause of death was officially recorded as carcinoma of the descending colon. He was 66, an early age for such an active man to be struck down. His wife Helena and their two daughters survived him.

The Times published an obituary in its edition of Friday 7 May 1948 together with a front page notice in the deaths column. Curiously, the date of death was given as 6 May and has been wrongly quoted in publications ever since. (A copy of the death certificate obtained from the Family Records Centre clearly shows both the date of death and date of notification as 5 May 1948.)

The funeral and service was held at Putney Vale Cemetery, about two miles from Wimbledon, on the morning of Saturday 8 May. A representative from the Robert Williams Group of Companies, for which Harry had worked for many years, attended the funeral but there was no military send off. It was mainly a family affair, which is what he would have

*Putney Vale Cemetery.
Harry Greenwood died
5 May 1948
and was buried in
plot 71c block N.
(photographs: Derek Hunt)*

wanted. He was buried in plot 71C, block N at Putney Vale, close to one of the internal roads. A pink granite headstone bears the inscription:

**TO
THE DEAREST MEMORY OF
HARRY GREENWOOD
VC. DSO. OBE. MC.
A DEVOTED HUSBAND AND FATHER
NOV 1881 - MAY 1948**

Many of the obituaries published at the time praised his outstanding bravery and his devotion to duty. Lieutenant-Colonel Harold E. Yeo MBE MC, writing in *The Bugle*, went further in summing up Harry Greenwood's character:

His was a vital personality, full of cheerful confidence in even the most difficult times. He always spoke and acted as if nothing were impossible to his company or battalion. This infectious enthusiasm, together with a remarkable gift for effective leadership in any crisis, resulted in a splendid unit which believed in itself and its commander; even the quite newly joined draft was quickly brought under the spell.

His death, after an illness borne with typical courage, removes another of those remarkable soldiers who spring from the ranks of Britain's civilian armies in every national emergency.

Chapter Twelve

Epilogue

Harry Greenwood did not write an autobiography or contribute to an official biography. He was a modest man and would not have considered his life exciting enough for others to take an interest. Consequently there was never any attempt to preserve letters, documents or diaries which would aid a biographer. Although the full story of his extraordinary life has not been published before he has been mentioned in several books, including the KOYLI Regimental History.

His last Will and Testament was dated 11 November 1947, less than six months before his untimely death. In the will Harry Greenwood, "A Lieutenant-Colonel in His Majesty's Army," appointed the Standard Bank of South Africa Ltd to act as executor and trustee and Messrs Maxwell Batley & Co of London E.C. to act as solicitors. Subject to the payment of debts, funeral and testamentary expenses his entire estate was bequeathed to Helena Greenwood. This had a gross value of £20,722-2s-3d (in excess of £450,000 in today's money) and a net value of £18,734-3s-7d after estate duty and other expenses. Probate was granted to the executor on 23 August 1948.

Helena Greenwood remained at 77 Home Park Road, Wimbledon for a few years after her husband's death. By 1951 the house had been converted into two flats, one of these being occupied by Cynthia and her husband Richard List. The house was later further converted into three flats and the Greenwood family moved out completely. For a while, during the early 1950s, Helena was living just up the road at 45 Home Park Road. Richard and Cynthia List emigrated to Canada in the 1950s, taking Helena Greenwood with them. Unfortunately, many of Harry Greenwood's personal records went missing at the time of the move.

Attempts to trace these records or anyone who knew the family when they lived in Wimbledon proved unsuccessful. As Cynthia List later told the author:

It is no wonder there was no information of us as a family in Wimbledon. We were only living there during the 1930s until war was declared, when my father was given The Pioneer Corps job and my mother, sister and I moved out. We moved back for only a few years after the war.

Richard List worked for many years for a Trust Company in Canada until he transferred to a new job with C&A in New York. They lived in Pelham, a suburb of New York, until Richard retired. He and Cynthia then moved

*A plaque was unveiled at Harry Greenwood's birthplace 8 April 1997.
(photograph: Derek Hunt)*

to Edmonds, Washington on the west coast of America to be near their daughters, one of whom lived in California and the other in Vancouver, Canada. Harry Greenwood's other daughter, Evelyn, was already living in the United States, having married Malcolm Onwood, an Englishman living in Massachusetts and returning there with him after the war.

Helena Greenwood never re-married. She remained in Canada after Cynthia and Richard moved to the USA and died at an advanced age, apparently well into her nineties. Nobody knew how old she really was as she did not seem too sure herself, and gave different ages when asked. She is buried in Canada.

In 1956 a Victoria Cross Centenary Exhibition was held at Marlborough House, London. The Exhibition (open from 15 June to 17 July) featured photographs and artefacts relating to 640 holders of the Victoria Cross. Harry Greenwood was represented by a photograph and VC citation loaned by The King's Own Yorkshire Light Infantry. Two souvenir booklets were published - one containing details of the exhibits and the other listing the VC citations.

Forty one years later the Royal Borough of Windsor and Maidenhead honoured the memory of Harry Greenwood VC by unveiling a plaque at his birthplace. Although he had died almost fifty years earlier his legend lived on, and when it was discovered that there was not already a plaque to him this omission was rectified. The blue plaque was fixed to the right of the main gates of Victoria Barracks, where it could be seen without entering the barracks. It was unveiled on Tuesday 8 April 1997 by the Mayor, Councillor Mrs Ady Sheldon. She paid the following tribute to Greenwood:

> *I am of French origin and my family comes from Alsace. This means that we have a great debt of gratitude to all the young men who fought in World War I and World War II. Without them and without the voice of Britain in occupied France we would have lost hope of recovering our freedom and the values which are dear to the democratic countries. I was therefore deeply moved to have this opportunity to pay tribute to someone who showed such bravery and to whom we owe so much.*

Guests at the ceremony included representatives from The Light Infantry (into which KOYLI had been merged in 1968) and the Victoria Cross and George Cross Association. Greenwood had never been a member of the VC & GC Association as it was established, in 1956, after his death. A reception was held in the officers' mess courtesy of the Scots Guards, then in residence at the barracks. Nothing remained of the building in which Greenwood was born as Victoria Barracks were demolished and rebuilt in the 1980s. Colonel Pat Porteous VC, who was awarded the Victoria Cross for outstanding gallantry and leadership at Dieppe in August 1942,

The plaque unveiling ceremony outside Victoria Barracks.
Left to right: Mrs Ady Sheldon, Mayor of the Royal Borough of Windsor and Maidenhead; Major Alastair Mathewson, Scots Guards; Colonel Pat Porteous VC.
(photograph: Windsor Express*)*

attended the ceremony. (Colonel Porteous, sadly, died in October 2000.) He said of Harry Greenwood:

> *I never met him but I am sure there were few who earned so many decorations in either of the two World Wars. He must have been a superb example to his battalion and all who knew him.*

The wording on the plaque reads:

Royal Borough of Windsor and Maidenhead
Lt. Col. Harry Greenwood VC DSO OBE MC
1881-1948
Born in Victoria Barracks
Awarded the Victoria Cross for bravery at
Ovillers, France in 1918 serving with the
King's Own Yorkshire Light Infantry

In the same year (1997) Putney Vale Cemetery named one of its internal roads after him. Wandsworth Council decided, in order to make it easier for visitors to find their way around the cemetery, to name the main pathways after the Victoria Cross holders buried there. The Cemetery is the final resting place of six VC holders, including Harry Greenwood, and there is a memorial to a seventh. 'Greenwood Road' is commemorated with road signs at either end, and a display relating to the Putney Vale VC holders was set up in the reception area near to the main entrance.

Greenwood Road, Putney Vale Cemetery. In 1997 Wandsworth Council named the main pathways in the cemetery after the Victoria Cross holders buried there. (photograph: Derek Hunt)

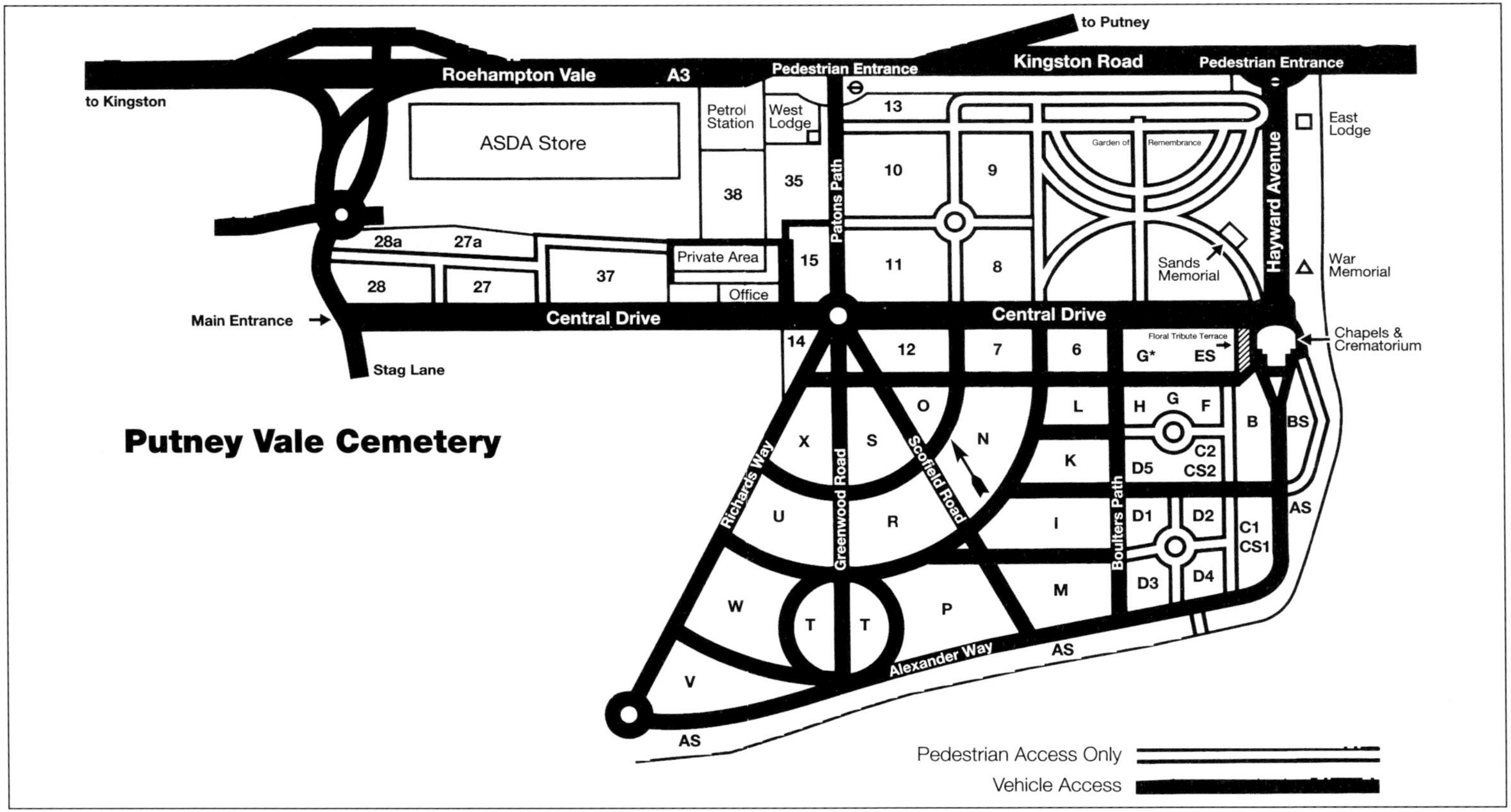

Harry Greenwood VC died 5 May 1948.
He is buried at Putney Vale Cemetery, Plot 71c Block N (position arrowed).
In 1997 Wandsworth Council named the main pathways in the cemetery after the Victoria Cross winners buried there.

Map reproduced by kind permission of Wandsworth Borough Council.

By 1999 the grave had become overgrown and in need of renovation. A local firm of stonemasons removed the earth and weeds from the centre of the grave and replaced with fresh grey granite chippings, and wire brushed the sides and also the headstone to remove moss. The renovation work was paid for by the Greenwood family.

The lives of three VC heroes connected with Windsor were commemorated in an exhibition in 1998. The Windsor Victoria Cross Exhibition, held at the historic Guildhall, was open to the public from 16 May to 31 May 1998.

Harry Greenwood was the second Windsor born man to be awarded the Victoria Cross. (The first was Alexander Hore-Ruthven, Sudan 1898, and the exhibition marked the centenary of his award.) The displays contained replica VCs and told the life stories of the local heroes, including details of how each man won his Victoria Cross. The King's Own Yorkshire Light Infantry Museum at Doncaster provided a number of exhibits, including a tunic similar to the one Lieutenant-Colonel Greenwood would have worn in 1918, officer's and other rank's field service caps, an 'active service' testament and several First World War photographs. Representatives from The Light Infantry attended the opening ceremony on Friday 15 May, which was also attended by two Second World War Victoria Cross recipients - Colonel Eric Wilson VC and Mr Tommy Gould VC. A souvenir brochure was produced for the event, with short biographies of Harry Greenwood and the two other Windsor VC recipients featured - Alexander Hore-Ruthven and Oliver Brooks.

In May 1998 the Windsor Victoria Cross Exhibition commemorated three VC recipients connected with Windsor - one of whom was Harry Greenwood.
(photograph: John Greenwood)

The KOYLI Museum, Doncaster kindly loaned a number of items to the Windsor Victoria Cross Exhibition, including the First World War Lieutenant-Colonel's tunic in the centre of the photograph. (photograph: John Greenwood)

The exhibition, which was officially opened by Lord Gowrie PC, the grandson of Alexander Hore-Ruthven VC, was well attended and proved popular with VC enthusiasts and the public. Many members of the Greenwood family also visited and loaned exhibits, including the CIV swagger cane. The display boards relating to Harry Greenwood VC are now owned by his family.

Only one of his three daughters is still alive. Mollie had died long ago in 1933 and Evelyn died in August 1998. At the time of writing (2003) Cynthia is living in California, USA.

Victoria Crosses continue to be much sought after by medal collectors, museums and also investors. In recent years the very scarcity of the VC has increased the prices realised at auction. Harry Greenwood's family, however, had long ago decided that his VC would never be sold. He bequeathed his VC and other medals, including miniatures, to his wife Helena, who in turn left them to their daughter Cynthia. Although kept in a bank vault for security reasons they were still treasured, along with the memory of a truly courageous member of "a fighting family." Cynthia List decided that it would be better for her father's medals to be displayed in a museum than gathering dust in a bank vault and planned to donate them to The King's Own Yorkshire Light Infantry Regimental Museum in Doncaster, South Yorkshire. She was not able to arrange this personally but her daughter, Anne Meagher, travelled to England from her home in Washington State, USA bringing the medals with her.

*Some of Harry Greenwood's medals, photographed for the Windsor Victoria Cross Exhibition, 1998.
Left to right: 1937 Coronation Medal, OBE, Victoria Cross, DSO and Bar, Military Cross, Queen's South Africa Medal,
King's South Africa Medal, 1914-15 Star, British War Medal 1914-20, Victory Medal.
(photograph: Cynthia List)*

*Harry Greenwood's medals being presented to the KOYLI Museum.
Left to right: Major Michael Deedes (Regimental Secretary KOYLI), John Greenwood (nephew),
Anne Meagher (granddaughter), Colonel Charles Greenwood (nephew).
(photograph: KOYLI Museum)*

At a private ceremony at the KOYLI Museum, attended by members of the Greenwood family and representatives from the regiment and the museum, Harry Greenwood's granddaughter handed the VC group over on 17 July 2002.

The medals, together with miniatures, were accepted on behalf of the museum by Major Michael Deedes, KOYLI Regimental Secretary. They were remounted and put on permanent display in the medals room. The museum now owns four of the nine VCs awarded to men serving in the regiment (see Appendix II). Major Deedes was quoted in the *Sheffield Star* - "He was as brave as they come. I am delighted that our museum now has Lieutenant-Colonel Greenwood's medals."

Two of Harry Greenwood's nephews, John Greenwood and Colonel Charles Greenwood, were at the museum to see the VC group being handed over. John Greenwood said "The medals have travelled half way round the world and I am very happy to see them finally displayed in the museum."

It is indeed a fitting tribute to this outstanding hero for his Victoria Cross and other gallantry awards to be owned by the regiment he loved so much, and which also loved him. He was ruthless in dealing with enemy machine-gun posts but was also a devoted family man and loved his country and the regiment in which he proudly served.

Harry Greenwood's VC group and miniatures on display at the KOYLI Museum, Doncaster.
(photograph: KOYLI Museum)

As L.D.S. (Captain Lancelot D. Spicer), a fellow KOYLI officer, noted in his obituary:

Infectious bubbling enthusiasm, fear for no man, respect for the traditional gods, happy and bountiful in his home and family life, all these made up the character of the man who earned the full-hearted admiration and often devotion of his fellow man. He fought three wars to defend the things he loved and in which he believed. St Peter can welcome and give high place to this Happy Warrior.

Appendix I

ORDERS, DECORATIONS AND MEDALS AWARDED TO HARRY GREENWOOD VC

Victoria Cross

Distinguished Service Order (DSO) and Bar

Officer, The Most Excellent Order of the British Empire (OBE)

Military Cross

Queen's South Africa Medal, with four clasps:
 (Cape Colony, Orange Free State, Johannesburg, Diamond Hill)

King's South Africa Medal, with two clasps:[1]
 (South Africa 1901 and South Africa 1902)

1914-15 Star

British War Medal 1914-20

Victory Medal, with MID Oakleaf

Defence Medal[2]

War Medal 1939-45[2]

King George V's Silver Jubilee Medal 1935[1]

King George VI's Coronation Medal 1937

---

1 These medals appear to have been self-awarded.

2 These medals were never claimed from the Ministry of Defence.

Appendix II

VICTORIA CROSS WINNERS OF THE KING'S OWN YORKSHIRE LIGHT INFANTRY

Private Charles Ward 2nd Battalion
South Africa, 1900

Major Charles Yate 2nd Battalion
France, 1914 (posthumous)

Lance-Corporal Frederick Holmes 2nd Battalion
France, 1914

Private Horace Waller 10th Battalion
France, 1917 (posthumous)

Sergeant John Ormsby 2nd Battalion
France, 1917

Private Wilfred Edwards 7th Battalion
Belgium, 1917

Lieutenant-Colonel Oliver Watson 2/5th Battalion
France, 1918 (posthumous)
(Lt. Col. Watson was commissioned into the Green Howards and was only temporarily posted to the KOYLI.)

Sergeant Laurence Calvert 5th Battalion
France, 1918

Lieutenant-Colonel Harry Greenwood 9th Battalion
France, 1918

The VC and medals for Wilfred Edwards, Harry Greenwood, John Ormsby and Charles Yate are held by The King's Own Yorkshire Light Infantry Museum, Doncaster.

Sources

The Canon W. M. Lummis VC Files, held at the National Army Museum (on behalf of the Military Historical Society) - the starting point for any VC research.
The Imperial War Museum.
The National Archives, Kew (see separate list).
Ministry of Defence, Defence Records, Hayes.
Ministry of Defence, Army Medal Office, Droitwich Spa.
Major C. M. J. Deedes, Regimental Secretary, Light Infantry Office (Yorkshire).
The King's Own Yorkshire Light Infantry Museum, Doncaster.
Joseph T. Warden, The Royal Logistic Corps Museum, Camberley.
Captain D. Mason, Regimental Archivist Grenadier Guards.
National Army Museum.
National Archives of South Africa.
South African Museum of Military History.
Register of Births, Marriages and Deaths.
The Met Office (formerly Meteorological Office).
Mrs Rita Read, Bruce Castle Museum, Tottenham.
Haringey Council Environmental Services.
The British Library Newspaper Library.
Wimbledon Library.
Windsor Library.
The Royal Borough Museum Collection.
Probate Registry, York.
Alan Barrett, Amenity Services Manager, Putney Vale Cemetery.
The Victoria Cross and George Cross Association.
Mrs Ady Sheldon, former Mayor of the Royal Borough of Windsor & Maidenhead.
Mrs Cynthia List, John Greenwood, Charles Greenwood, Roland Greenwood and Mrs Patricia Roberts for their personal reminiscences and many photographs.
Mr Dorien Clifford - for his topographical descriptions of the French battlefields, particularly around Ovillers, the photographs he took on his visits and for producing many of the maps used.
Alan Jordan and Bob Wyatt - for their technical advice.
Mrs Rosamond Nicholls - for her personal reminiscences.
Colonel Paul Oldfield - for sharing information gathered while writing his book about the British VC winners of the Western Front.
Mlle Claudine Pardon - for photographs of Ovillers.
Mrs Carol Scott - for copies of documents relating to the 1920 VC Garden Party.
Mr J. V. Webb - for his willingness to share his wide knowledge of the CIV.

Whilst every effort has been made to trace the copyright holders or the photographers of illustrations used this has not always proved possible. Should anyone feel that a photograph has been used without proper accreditation would they please contact the publisher.

Documents held at the National Archives, Kew (formerly the Public Record Office)

WO 95/2133	War Diaries 21st Division (January - August 1918)
WO 95/2134	War Diaries 21st Division (September 1918 - March 1919)
WO 95/2159	War Diaries 64th Infantry Brigade (July 1915 - May 1917)
WO 95/2160	War Diaries 64th Infantry Brigade (June 1917 - March 1919)
WO 95/2161	War Diaries 15th Bn. Durham Light Infantry and War Diaries 1st Bn. East Yorkshire Regiment
WO 95/2162	War Diaries 9th Bn. KOYLI & War Diaries 10th Bn. KOYLI
WO 95/2163	War Diaries 110th Infantry Brigade
WO 95/2164	War Diaries 7th & 8th Bns. Leicestershire Regiment
WO 95/2421	War Diaries 19th Infantry Brigade
WO 95/2422	War Diaries 5th /6th Scottish Rifles
WO 97/2928	Attestation forms for Charles Greenwood
WO 253/5	War Record No. 12 Pioneer Corps Holding & Training Unit
	Various Medal Rolls

Newspapers and Publications

African World London
Daily Sketch
Sheffield Star
The Star Johannesburg
The Times
Tottenham and Edmonton Weekly Herald
Walsall Observer
Wimbledon Borough News
Windsor & Eton Express
Windsor & Maidenhead Observer
The Bugle Journal of The King's Own Yorkshire Light Infantry
The Pioneer Journal of the Royal Pioneer Corps

The Royal Logistic Corps Journal
The Silver Bugle Journal of The Light Infantry
Soldier

Army Lists
Benguela Railway booklet
Kelly's Directory
The London Gazette
Medal News
Who's Who/Who was Who

Bibliography

Bond, R. C., Lt. Col.
History of the King's Own Yorkshire Light Infantry in the Great War 1914-1918
Percy Lund, Humphries & Co Ltd 1929

Creagh, Sir O'Moore & Humphris, E. M.
The Distinguished Service Order
Standard Art Book Co. Ltd, London 1924

Edmonds, Sir James, Brigadier-General.
History of the Great War. Military Operations France & Belgium 1914-1918
HMSO 1922-1949

Gliddon, Gerald.
VCs of the First World War. Spring Offensive 1918.
Sutton Publishing, Stroud 1997

Gliddon, Gerald.
VCs of the First World War. The Final Days 1918
Sutton Publishing, Stroud 2000

James, E. A.
British Regiments 1914-1918
Naval & Military Press, Heathfield

Johnson, J. H.
1918 The Unexpected Victory
Arms & Armour Press, London 1997

Mackinnon, W. H., Major-General.
The Journal of the CIV in South Africa
John Murray, 1901.

Moore, Geoffrey.
Pickman's Progress in the City Imperial Volunteers in South Africa 1900.
Published privately

Pillinger, Dennis & Staunton, Anthony.
Victoria Cross Presentations and Locations
Published privately 2000

Rhodes-Wood, E. H., Major.
A War History of the Royal Pioneer Corps 1939-1945
Details not known

This England Books
The Register of the Victoria Cross
Cheltenham 1997

Wilson, H. W.
With the Flag to Pretoria (2 vols)
Harmsworth Brothers Ltd, London 1900

Wilson, H. W.
After Pretoria: The Guerilla War (2 vols)
The Amalgamated Press Ltd, London 1902

History of the Great War. Order of Battle of Divisions Part 3a New Army Divisions (9-26)
No Author

Medal Yearbook 2002
Token Publishing Ltd, Honiton

A Short History of the King's Own Yorkshire Light Infantry 1755-1965. **No Author. Wakefield Express Series Ltd**

The Times History of the War
The Times, London

The Transvaal in Peace & War 1900
No details

Victoria Cross Centenary Exhibition 1856-1956
HMSO 1956

For a list of books relating to Harry Greenwood VC please see
Victoria Cross Bibliography
by John Mulholland and Alan Jordan.
Spink, London 1999

Index

Aisne, Battle of the 50
Allenby, First Viscount 107
Amerval 64, 67-8, 70-1
Anderson, Daniel 18, 20
Annand VC, Captain R. W. vii
Arras, Battle of 38, 51
Asquith, Herbert 42

Baden-Powell, Major-General Robert 15
Battery Valley 57-9
Benguela Railway 98, 100-3
Bois le Due (Dukes Wood) 65, 74, 76, 79, 87,
Boom Ravine 57, 59-61
British Expeditionary Force 21-2, 30, 111
Broodseinde, Battle of 39, 41
Brooks VC, Oliver 122, 132
Butt, Sir Alfred 93

Caldwell VC, CSM Thomas 92-3
Calvert VC, Sergeant Laurence 122-3
Chamberlain, Neville 104, 111
Churchill, Winston 15, 90, 111
Cruickshank VC, Private Robert 89

Daniell, Lieutenant-Colonel N.R. 38-9
Daykins VC, Sergeant John 92-3
Deedes, Major Michael 135
Diamond Hill, Transvaal 13, 14
Dill, Lieutenant-Colonel RC. 22
Doyle VC, CSM John 92-3

Edwards, Brigadier-General CV. 74, 79, 82, 85, 91

Fields, Gracie 115
French, Field Marshal Viscount Sir John 21, 30, 37, 88

George V, King 18, 30, 42, 52, 89, 91-2, 95-6, 98, 109
George VI, King 109, 121
Gould VC, Tommy 132
Grand Gay Farm 66, 80, 82, 87
Greenwood, Alice Stella Evelyn (daughter of HG) 20, 37-9, 105, 108, 113-4, 122, 128, 133
Greenwood, Arthur (brother of HG) 7, 23, 26-7, 33, 35, 105, 107-8, 114, 123
Greenwood, Charles (father of HG) 2-4, 6-8, 12, 18, 23, 26, 33-4, 89, 104-5
Greenwood, Charles (brother of HG) 7, 35, 115
Greenwood, Charles and John (nephews of HG) 107-8, 132-3, 135
Greenwood, David (brother of HG) 7, 26-7, 35, 99, 114
Greenwood, Harry
  Award of VC 1, 74-80, 82, 85-94
  Award of DSO 1, 49, 52-3
  Award of Bar to DSO 1, 62
  Award of OBE 117
  Award of MC 1, 30
  Award of Mention in Despatches 32, 37, 88-9, 92-3
  Award of Boer War Medals 16-17
  Award of 1935 Jubilee Medal 109
  Award of 1937 Coronation Medal 109
  Birth 3-4
  Boer War service 9-18
  Business interests 17, 20, 98-104
  Cadet Battalion service 8, 11
  Children 20, 22, 24-5, 38-9, 52, 133
  Commissioned 22, 24
  Demobilised 91-2
  Death, funeral, burial 124-6, 131
  Donation of VC and medals 133-6
  Early life 2-8

Family relationships 2-7, 18, 26-27, 33-5, 99, 104-9, 113-4, 122-4, 127-8
First World War service 21-94
Inter-war years 95-109
Investitures 52, 88, 91-3, 104
KOYLI service 22-136
Marriage 18-20
Pioneer Corps service 112-120
Plaque 128-130
Post War years 121-6
Promotions 30, 32, 42-3, 51-3, 117, 122
Second World War service 111-120
Unknown Warrior Service 96, 98
VC Garden Party 95-7
Wounds 57, 61, 82, 89
Greenwood, Harry (son of HG) 20, 24-5, 105, 124
Greenwood, Helena (née Anderson, wife of HG) 18-20, 35, 38-9, 52, 91-2, 96, 98-9, 104-5, 113-4, 122-4, 127-8
Greenwood, John (brother of HG) 7, 23, 26-7, 35, 99, 114
Greenwood, Kate (Kitty, sister of HG) 7, 52, 99, 104, 114
Greenwood, Margaret (née Abernethy, mother of HG) 2, 6, 7, 18, 23-4, 26, 99 104-5
Greenwood, Mary Ann (daughter of Charles and Margaret Greenwood) 7, 24
Greenwood, Mollie Helena Margaret (daughter of HG) 20, 22, 35, 52, 104-5, 124, 133
Greenwood, Violet Cynthia Marion (daughter of HG) 20, 52, 91-2, 101, 105, 113, 122-3, 127, 133

Haig, Field Marshal Sir Douglas 25, 30, 39, 43, 88
Hamilton, Major-General Bruce 12
Headlam, Brigadier-General H.R. 51, 53
Heathcote, Lieutenant-Colonel C.E. 37
Hindenburg, Field Marshal 38, 84
Hitler, Adolf 104, 111, 117

Holmes VC, Captain Frederick 122-3
Hore-Ruthven VC, Alexander 4, 132, 133

King's Own Yorkshire Light Infantry Museum, Doncaster 12, 17, 132-3, 135-6
Kipling, Rudyard 7
Kitchener, Lord 8-9, 15, 22, 42
Kruger, Paul 9

List, Richard 123, 127
Lloyd George, David 42-3
Lobito Bay, West Africa 99, 101-2
Loos 25, 28-29, 30-2, 51
Lucas VC, Charles xi
Ludendorff, General Erich 43, 47, 50, 54, 84
Lynch, Lieutenant-Colonel Colmer W.D. 24, 33, 36
Lys, Battle of the 47

Mackinnon, Colonel W.H. 11, 15
McCulloch, Lieutenant-Colonel Andrew J. (later Brigadier-General) 42-3, 47, 49-51, 53, 57, 60
Meagher, Anne (granddaughter of HG) 133, 135
Milward, Lieutenant-Colonel C.A. 37
Montgomery, Field Marshal Viscount 107
Mountbatten, Lord 117

Neuvilly 67-8
Newton, Sir Alfred 12
Nicholas VC, Private Henry 52
Nicholls, Rosamond 123

Onwood, Malcolm Brooks 122, 128
Ovillers 22, 63-5, 67, 69-77

Passchendaele 39, 43, 84
Poix du Nord 66, 77-79, 82
Porteous VC, Colonel Pat 129-130
Prince of Wales (later Edward VIII) 98
Probyn VC, General Sir Dighton 96

Rhodes, Cecil 17, 20
Roberts VC, Field Marshal Lord 8-9, 12, 14, 15

Scott, Colonel C.J. 118
Sheldon, Mrs Ady, Mayor of Windsor and Maidenhead 129
Somme, Battle of the 36-9, 51, 84
Spicer, Lieutenant Lancelot Dykes (later Captain Spicer, DSO, MC and Bar) 24, 60, 90, 136

Tewfik, Khedive 6
Towers VC, Private James 92-3

Vendegies-au-Bois 64-5, 75-7, 82
Victoria, Queen xi, 2, 4, 7, 88
Victoria Cross xi, 1, 17, 25, 52, 74, 79, 82, 84-96, 98, 124, 130, 132-3, 135
Victoria Cross Centenary Exhibition, (1956), 128
Victoria Cross Dinner, The Dorchester, (1946) 122
Victoria Cross Garden Party, (1920) 95-7
Victory Parade, (1946) 121

Walsh, Major Theobald Alfred 60-2, 85, 90
Williams, Sir Robert 17, 20, 98-9, 101-2, 104, 124
Wilson VC, Colonel Eric 132
Wilson, Woodrow 84
Windsor Infantry Barracks (Victoria Barracks) 2-5, 128-130
Windsor Victoria Cross Exhibition vi, 132-3
Wolseley, Lord 9
Wright, Private H. 46, 49

Yeo, Lieutenant Harold E. (later Lieutenant-Colonel, MBE MC) 24, 126